To my children Arnaav, Mansi and Ansh,
my papa and my mummy watching from her
heavenly abode.

About STEM For Kids

Mission: Make STEM fun and real.

STEM For Kids® is the brainchild of Moni Singh. After contributing as an engineer and an industry leader to the development and deployment of various technologies like wireless phones, telecommunications equipment and smart meters, Singh embarked on the mission to expose children to the immense potential, the energy and the excitement in STEM fields.

Her two children, a 1st and a 2nd grader at that time, were Singh's inspirations. One day, making paper bridges with them, she noticed the spark in their eyes as they engineered new and stronger bridge designs. Not only were they deeply engaged, they were hungry for more. Seeing their craving for more hands-on STEM activities, Singh tried to find programs in the area but to no avail. Singh was determined to do something to keep the spark alive for her kids and to create more sparks in young minds in the community. STEM For Kids® was born.

Born and raised with industry, STEM For Kids® is unique in its strong ties to the real world of STEM. Programs are designed by engineers, people in the industry & educators to specifically address "so what" in a hands-on way. An equal emphasis is placed on keeping the programs fun and exciting so children may develop an intrinsic interest in STEM.

The STEM For Kids® curriculum has evolved to over 40 different courses used by thousands of educators serving millions of children worldwide. Like Singh's now 2nd grader (yes! her third child), many generation Alpha kids continue the fun-filled STEM learning experiences.

Scan the QR Code to Access Helpful Materials To Enhance Your STEM Teaching Experience!

This STEM Instruction Manual Issued To:

_____

IMPORTANT NOTICE:

ISBN: 978-1-971346-00-7

Table of Contents

Mechanical Engineering: Motion & Machine Makers

STEM For Kids® "Motion & Machine Makers" is your comprehensive instructor manual for introducing the dynamic world of mechanical engineering and Newton's laws of motion to PreK-5 learners. Mechanical engineering is the backbone of our modern world. It is the force behind the cars we drive, the medical robots that save lives, and the sustainable energy systems protecting our planet. In an increasingly automated world, understanding how things move and function is a foundational skill.

This resource provides engaging, hands-on activities, design challenges, and real-world scenarios that make engineering concepts accessible and exciting while fostering critical thinking, creativity, collaboration, and problem-solving skills. From building grabbers to designing cars and testing balancing devices, this guide provides practical strategies to help your students master the fundamentals of forces and machines.

Educational Connection

STEM For Kids 4 Dimensional Learning		
Core Ideas *(Standards - what it is)*	*Career Connections & Practices* *(CCP - what to do)*	*Cross-Cutting Concepts* *(CCC - how it relates)*
Science Standards: • Algorithms and Coding • Motion and Stability: Forces and Interactions • Matter and Its interactions • Engineering Design Information & Communications Technology (ICT): • Computer Systems • Technology as a Tool • Data and Analysis • Networks and the Internet Applied Mathematics: • Make sense of problems and persevere in solving them • Reason abstractly and quantitatively • Look for and make use of structure Applied Language Arts: • Comprehension and collaboration • Presentation of Knowledge and Ideas	Critical Thinking: • Analyze how forces, motion, and inertia impact real-world machines and structures. • Predict the outcomes of experiments and adjust strategies based on observed results. • Interpret data from tests, such as force needed to move a car, rocket speed, or friction experiments, to inform improvements. Research: • Investigate real-life machines and their mechanical properties. • Explore the history of inventions, including the work of engineers like Leonardo da Vinci. Collaboration: • Work in teams to design, build, and test projects such as human roller coasters, balancing devices, or bouncy houses. • Share responsibilities in group experiments and collectively troubleshoot design challenges. • Communicate results and present findings to peers for feedback and discussion. Creativity: • Brainstorm and design innovative machines and devices using available materials. • Develop unique solutions to engineering challenges. • Apply creative thinking to improve motion, stability, and efficiency in design projects. • Work creatively together with a group of participants. Communication: • Present project designs, experiment results, and improvements clearly to peers and instructors. • Explain reasoning behind design choices and the application of motion concepts. • Document testing processes, observations, and outcomes for analysis and reflection. Problem Solving: • Apply the engineering design process to define goals, plan, create, test, and improve mechanisms. • Troubleshoot challenges related to motion, force, inertia, and friction in hands-on projects. • Use iterative testing and refinement to overcome obstacles and optimize designs.	Systems & Models: • Understand how mechanical systems and machines work together to perform a function or action. • Examine how individual components influence the overall performance of a device. • Explore models of motion, force, and energy to predict outcomes in engineering projects. Structure & Function: • Identify the relationship between a machine's design and purpose. • Understand how materials, shape, and construction affect stability, strength, and motion. • Examine how engineers optimize machines to perform tasks efficiently. • Evaluate real-world mechanisms. Patterns: • Recognize recurring behaviors in motion, force, and mechanical performance. • Identify trends in how design changes affect efficiency and effectiveness. • Observe patterns in experiments to predict outcomes of solutions. • Track repeated results to refine understanding of mechanical principles and improve designs. Scale, Proportion, & Quantity: • Compare sizes, weights, and forces to determine balance, stability, and motion. • Analyze proportional relationships in design elements to optimize function. • Apply measurements and calculations to predict outcomes in challenges. • Adjust scale and quantity of materials to achieve desired mechanical performance.

Career Connections:	Cause & Effect:
• Explore roles of mechanical engineers and related STEM jobs. • Understand how engineers solve practical problems using physics, materials, and design thinking. • Examine how the skills learned - critical thinking, collaboration, and problem-solving - transfer to real-world engineering jobs.	• Examine how applying force affects motion and stability. • Analyze the results of design decisions to improve machine function. • Understand how changes to materials, structure, or motion lead to different outcomes. • Predict and test the impact of engineering solutions through hands-on experiments.

Social Emotional Learning(how it feels)

Engage students in hands-on mechanical engineering projects to explore motion, forces, and friction while developing self-awareness, collaboration, problem-solving, and emotional resilience.

STEM For Kids + ECERS: What We Support

1. A Rich, Child-Centered Environment
   - Children's creations are proudly displayed at their eye level.
   - Hands-on STEM projects show each child's unique ideas and creativity.
   - We include 3D builds, models, and displays that connect to current themes.

2. Warm, Supportive Relationships
   - Staff help children jump right into activities with confidence.
   - We build strong communication with families throughout the program.

3. Choice-Based Small Groups
   - Teachers guide learning, but kids take the lead in creating, building, and exploring.

4. Language, Literacy & Problem-Solving in Action
   - STEM topics come alive through books, pictures, and puppets.
   - Children talk, share ideas, and explain their thinking throughout the day.
   - We ask "how?", "why?", and "what do you think?" to build reasoning skills.
   - Kids turn their ideas into words through whiteboarding, storytelling, and engineers' talk.

5. Fine Motor Skills Through Hands-On Making
   - Lego builds, tools, art supplies, and manipulatives strengthen precision and coordination.
   - Kids cut, tape, design, connect, and build using real materials.

6. Creative Arts Integrated Into STEM
   - Children explore drawing, painting, building, collage, and sculpting.
   - Activities encourage individual creativity while connecting to STEM themes.
   - Music, dance, and movement are woven into lessons (e.g., scientific songs and motion games).

7. Play-Based Exploration Across All Learning Areas
   - **Blocks:** Build, test, and learn about stability and forces.
   - **Water/Sand:** Explore hydropower, waterproofing, dirtproofing, and more.
   - **Dramatic Play:** Role-play careers like doctors, engineers, scientists, and inventors.
   - **Nature & Science:** Investigate real objects, observe weather, explore shadows and insects.
   - **Math & Numbers:** Count, measure, compare, graph, sort, categorize, and use shapes.

8. Purposeful Use of Technology
   - Videos and digital tools encourage active thinking and doing.
   - Staff stay engaged—asking questions, guiding exploration, and connecting concepts to the theme.

9. Inclusion & Diversity
   - Materials, stories, and activities celebrate diverse people and experiences.
   - Children see themselves and others reflected positively in the curriculum.

10. Strong Supervision & Supportive Interactions
    - Staff stay aware and present, ensuring safe, meaningful play.
    - Encouragement, warmth, and respect guide every interaction.
    - Children collaborate, communicate, and build social skills through team challenges.
    - Plenty of materials and choices reduce conflict and build cooperation.

"Motion & Machine Makers" lays the groundwork for technical literacy, ensuring the next generation of engineers is equipped with both physical building skills and the digital intelligence to lead.

Foundational STEM Coaching Resources

Please use the STEM For Kids® The STEM Coaching Manual as the foundational resource for how to bring STEM education to the students in your classroom.

Here is a list of common topics from **The STEM Coaching Manual** for your reference. These are subject to change. Kindly refer to the Manual for the latest:

Foundations of STEM Coaching ○ About STEM For Kids ○ The STEM Way	**STEM For Kids 4 Dimensional Learning** ○ What it is ○ Career Connections & Practices ○ Cross-Cutting Concepts

Planning and Preparation
○ Five Key Points of STEM Coaching
○ Course Training
○ Classroom Management
○ Frequently Asked Questions
	Conducting the Program
	○ Checklists & Responsibilities
	  ■ First Day
	  ■ Conducting Activities During A Class
	  ■ Middle of Program
	  ■ End of Program
	○ Setting Children's Expectations
	○ Accentuating Key Learnings
	○ Customizing Program Delivery
	○ Scaling Up or Down Activities
	○ Parental/Community Engagement & Communications
	○ Specific Activities for First Day, During the Program, and Last Day

Student Project Evaluation and Success
 	
○ Assessment Reports
  ■ Engineering Design Project Assessment
  ■ Teamwork Assessment
  ■ Social Emotional Learning Assessment
○ Student Peer Review
○ Pre- and Post- Attitude Surveys
○ Certificate of Completion	

Important Guidelines for Delivering the Curriculum:

- Keep it fun and feel free to get into the fun yourself.
- Be a coach: enquire about children's thinking and encourage them to think in new ways.
- Listen for ideas from children.
- Encourage everyone's participation. Use children volunteers when you can.
- Start each day with a playful way to recap what children did previously (ideas are provided in the Ways to Recap section).
- End each day with a recap of main themes from the day.
- Use simple, age appropriate, language for describing the complex science and engineering concepts (each activity module provides you with guidelines and recommended way to approach a concept)
- Make kids curious and tap into that curiosity for maximum learning impact. Use best practices provided here and in the STEM Coaching Manual to arouse curiosity.

Any media (video and pictures) referenced throughout this book are provided in the STEM For Kids' STEM Coaches Member Area. For more information about membership and a free sampling of some of the available resources, visit **https://teach4d.stemforkids.net/start-free**.

The worksheets referenced throughout this instructional manual are available in the STEM For Kids® **Mechanical Engineering: Motion & Machine Makers Student's Workbook.**

Beginning the Program

At the beginning of each program, it is important that you outline the program expectations and how you expect participants to act throughout the various activities. Part of this beginning process involves having children introduce themselves in a fun, camp-like manner. Expectations will differ from program to program; however introductions, warm-up activities, and ice-breakers should be a part of a program's first day. This section will give you some ideas for how to do that. You are not limited to these activities.

Here are some common Beginning the Program Checklist items from **The STEM Coaching Manual**

Step 0	(Optional) Before the program starts, send a communique to the parents to set learning expectations and any needed logistical information.
Step 1	Complete the Walk-in and Drop Off procedures. Note and complete any additional procedures for the site.
Step 2	Complete the Pre-Assessment Attitude Survey with the participants.
Step 3	Pick one or two Introduction Games to conduct with the participants.
Step 4	Discuss the participant Expectations, Rewards and Consequences. Recall the 5 key points of STEM Coaching.
Step 5	(Optional) Conduct a Warm-Up Activity on the first day or any time children need to re-charge / re-focus.
Step 6	Conduct Internet Safety activities when working with the internet in a program.
Step 7	Do the Conducting Activities During a Class checklist throughout the day as you are going through your activities with the children.
Step 8	Leverage the STEM For Kids 4 Dimensional Learning Methodology by fostering Career Connections & Practices (CCPs) and exploring Cross-Cutting Concepts (CCCs) to inspire innovative thinking. Enquire about their thought processes, challenge them to consider new perspectives, and connect their learning to real-world applications and careers.
Step 9	Have fun! Allow the children to explore and learn in a low stress environment. Take pictures and videos throughout the day of the participants and full group, if applicable.
Step 10	RECAP RECAP RECAP. Complete Recap games throughout the day to promote key learning.
Step 11	Complete the Pick-Up and Location Close Out procedures per Daily Checklist. Note and complete any site specific procedures. Complete first day of program parent communique.

During the Program

During each program, it is essential to revisit and reinforce previously learned material to ensure long-term retention and deeper understanding. Regular review sessions help students connect new concepts with prior knowledge, fostering a stronger foundation for future learning. **The STEM Coaching Manual** offers a variety of engaging strategies and activities to facilitate this process, from interactive discussions to hands-on games.

However, feel free to adapt or introduce new methods that best suit the needs and dynamics of your students. The goal is to create meaningful opportunities for reflection and application, enhancing both confidence and competence as students progress through the program.

Here are some common During the Program Checklist items from **The STEM Coaching Manual**.

Step 1	Complete the Walk-in and Drop Off procedures. Note and complete any additional procedures for the site.
Step 2	Discuss the participant Expectations, Rewards and Consequences. Recall the 5 key points of STEM Coaching.
Step 3	(Optional) Conduct a Warm-Up Activity any time energy needs to be released.
Step 4	RECAP RECAP RECAP. Complete Recap games at the beginning of the day based on what concepts they learned the day before and on previous days.
Step 5	Do the Conducting Activities During a Class checklist throughout the day as you are going through your activities with the children.
Step 6	Leverage the STEM For Kids 4 Dimensional Learning Methodology by fostering Career Connections & Practices (CCPs) and exploring Cross-Cutting Concepts (CCCs) to inspire innovative thinking. Enquire about their thought processes, challenge them to consider new perspectives, and connect their learning to real-world applications and careers.
Step 7	Have fun! Allow the children to explore and learn in a low stress environment. Take pictures and videos throughout the day of the participants and full group, if applicable.
Step 8	RECAP RECAP RECAP. Complete Recap games at the end of the day based on what concepts they learned that day and on previous days.
Step 9	Complete the Pick-Up and Location Close Out procedures per Daily Checklist. Note and complete any site specific procedures. Complete middle of program parent communique.

Ending the Program

As the program concludes, it's important to celebrate achievements and reinforce learning through reflection, feedback, and recognition. Encourage participants to share their experiences and showcase their work to build confidence and strengthen their understanding. Incorporate activities that review key concepts, promote collaboration, and gather valuable insights on their growth. Providing opportunities for recognition and personal expression ensures a meaningful and lasting impact as participants complete the program.

Here are some common Ending the Program Checklist items from **The STEM Coaching Manual**.

Step 1	Complete the Walk-in and Drop Off procedures. Note and complete any additional procedures for the site.
Step 2	Discuss the participant Expectations, Rewards and Consequences. Recall the 5 key points of STEM Coaching.
Step 3	Use the During the Program Checklist.
Step 4	Have the participants show and tell the learning & projects they did in the program to parents and others.
Step 5	Complete the Post-Assessment Survey with the participants. Conduct Peer Feedback, Completion of Course Certificate, and Camper's Talk with the participants.
Step 6	RECAP RECAP RECAP. Complete Recap games at the end of the day based on what concepts they learned throughout the week.
Step 7	Complete the Pick-Up and Location Close Out procedures per Daily Checklist. Note and complete any site specific procedures. Complete last day parent communique.

STEM *for kids*

INVENTOR NAME(S): _____

_____

INVENTION DATE: _____

UNIQUE DESIGN QUALITIES PATENTED:

PATENT NO. _ _ _ _ _ _

SIGNATURE OF INVENTOR(S): _____

_____

SIGNATURE OF ISSUER: _____

STEM *for kids*

INVENTOR NAME(S): _____

_____

INVENTION DATE: _____

UNIQUE DESIGN QUALITIES PATENTED:

PATENT NO. _ _ _ _ _ _

SIGNATURE OF INVENTOR(S): _____

_____

SIGNATURE OF ISSUER: _____

STEMtastic Projects Registration Office

The undersigned hereby submit these Articles of Organization for the purpose of working together as a team in a class project.

The name of the company is: _____

The project that we will do together is: _____

_____

_____

_____

The company will automatically dissolve at the completion of the project activity.

The name and role of each person completing this Articles of Organization is as follows (list every team member's first name and their role):

First Name Only	Role

These articles will be effective upon filing.

Today is the _____ day of _____, _____.
    (number of the day)   *(name of the month)*   *(year)*

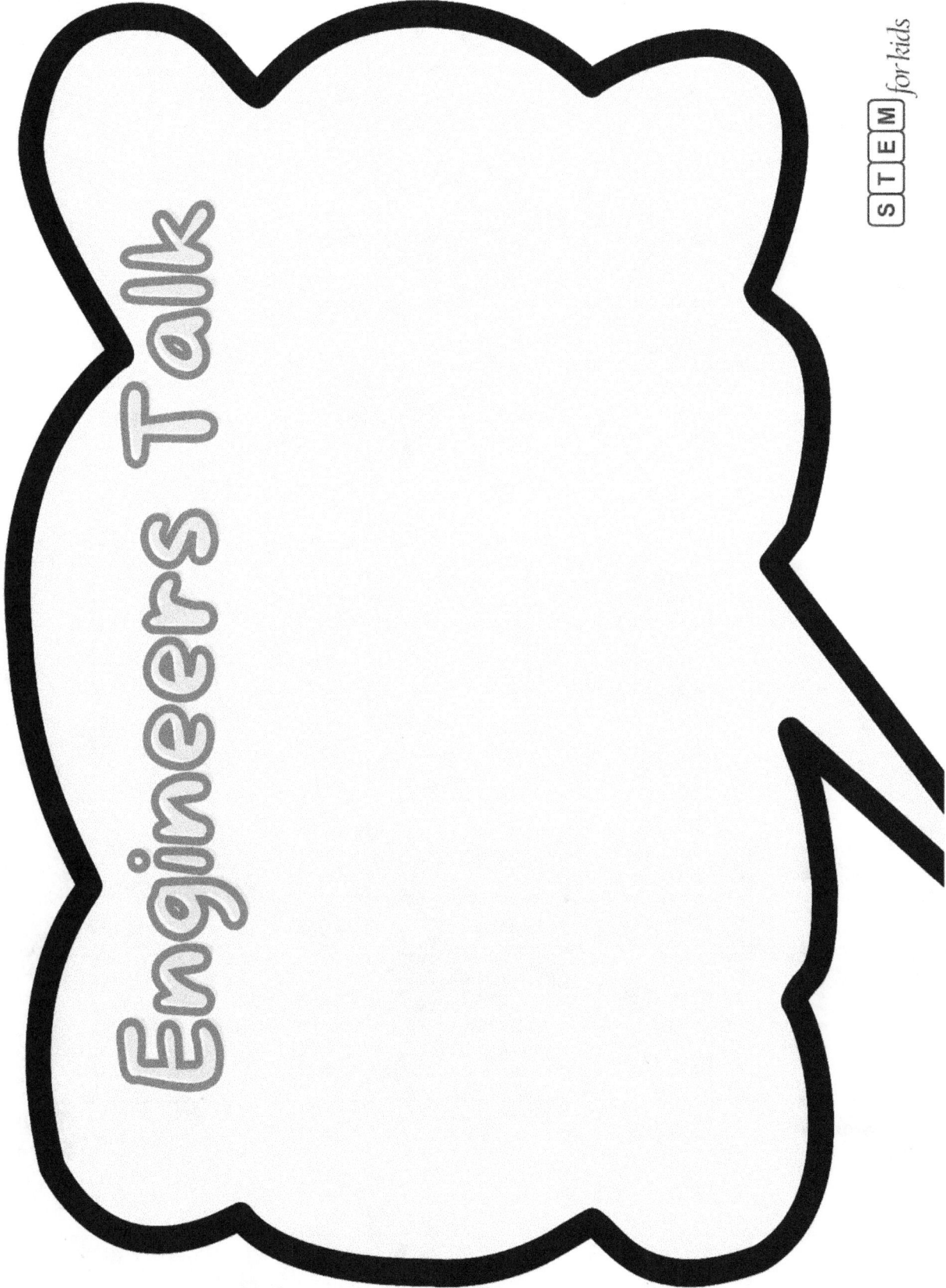

Engineers Talk

Engineering Design Project Assessment

Use the provided Engineering Design Project Rubric to assess student understanding of the project or to grade the project for classroom usage.

Project Name:					
	1 (Does Not Meet Expectations)	**2** (Approaches Expectations)	**3** (Meets Expectations)	**4** (Exceeds Expectations)	**Score** (Out of 4)
Critical Thinking	Does not identify the problem or constraints.	Has difficulty identifying the problem or constraints.	Identifies the problem and some constraints.	Clearly identifies the problem and constraints.	
Design Process	Does not follow the design process.	Struggles to follow the design process.	Follows the design process with some gaps.	Follows the design process (ask, imagine, plan, create, improve) effectively.	
Creativity	Design is unoriginal and lacks creativity.	Design lacks creativity.	Demonstrates some creativity in the design.	Demonstrates a high level of creativity in the design.	
Functionality	The project does not meet the basic requirements of the challenge.	Project is not functionally sound.	Project is functionally sound but may have minor flaws.	Project is functionally sound and meets all the requirements of the challenge.	
Efficiency	Project is extremely inefficient in terms of materials and time.	Project is inefficient in terms of materials or time.	Project is reasonably efficient in terms of materials and time.	Project is efficient in terms of materials used and creation time.	
Presentation	Does not present the design process, results, and conclusions.	Struggles to present the design process, results, and conclusions.	Presents the design process, results, and conclusions with some clarity.	Clearly and effectively presents the design process, results, and conclusions.	
Feedback:					**Total Score:**

Teamwork Assessment

Use the provided Teamwork Rubric to assess student understanding of the project or to grade the project for classroom usage.

Project Name:

	1 (Does Not Meet Expectations)	2 (Approaches Expectations)	3 (Meets Expectations)	4 (Exceeds Expectations)	Score (Out of 4)
Active Participation	Rarely participates in team activities or contributes to discussions.	Participates in some team activities, but may be passive or disengaged.	Contributes to team discussions and decision-making, but may be less assertive.	Actively participates in all team discussions and decision-making processes.	
Effective Communication	Rarely communicates with team members or struggles to express ideas clearly.	Communicates with team members, but may have difficulty expressing ideas or listening to others.	Communicates effectively with team members, but may have occasional misunderstandings.	Communicates clearly and effectively with team members, both verbally and in writing.	
Conflict Resolution	Avoids conflict or escalates conflicts in a destructive manner.	May struggle to resolve conflicts or may resort to passive-aggressive behavior.	Handles conflicts respectfully and attempts to find compromises.	Actively seeks to resolve conflicts peacefully and collaboratively.	
Respect for Others	Disregards the opinions and contributions of others.	May be dismissive of others' ideas or contributions.	Generally respects others, but may have occasional disagreements.	Demonstrates respect for the ideas, opinions, and contributions of all team members.	
Teamwork	Rarely works collaboratively or undermines the team's efforts.	May have difficulty working collaboratively or may hinder the team's progress.	Contributes to the team's success, but may not always be fully engaged.	Works effectively as part of a team to achieve common goals.	
Shared Responsibility	Does not contribute to the team's workload and avoids taking responsibility.	May avoid taking responsibility or may contribute unequally to the team's workload.	Contributes to the team's workload, but may rely on others for support.	Takes ownership of their responsibilities and contributes equally to the team's workload.	

Feedback:

Total Score:

Social Emotional Learning Assessment

Use the provided Social Emotional Learning Rubric to evaluate and support the development of participants' social & emotional skills in the program.

Project Name:

	1 (Does Not Meet Expectations)	2 (Approaches Expectations)	3 (Meets Expectations)	4 (Exceeds Expectations)	Score (Out of 4)
Persistence	Shows little effort or persistence in completing the project.	May give up easily when faced with difficulties.	Persists through challenges, but may require occasional encouragement.	Demonstrates a high level of persistence and resilience in overcoming challenges.	
Time Management	Consistently misses deadlines and fails to complete the project.	Struggles to manage time effectively and may miss deadlines.	Completes the project on time, but may have occasional delays.	Effectively manages time and resources to complete the project on schedule.	
Work Ethic	Consistently fails to meet expectations in terms of work ethic.	Lacks organization and attention to detail.	Demonstrates a good work ethic, but may have occasional lapses.	Exhibits a strong work ethic, including punctuality, organization, and attention to detail.	
Initiative	Shows little initiative or interest in the project.	Relies heavily on instructions and guidance from others.	Shows initiative and willingness to take on additional responsibilities.	Takes initiative and goes above and beyond the requirements of the project.	
Quality of Work	Produces work that is clearly below standard.	Produces work that is incomplete or contains errors.	Produces good-quality work that is generally accurate and complete.	Produces high-quality work that is accurate, complete, and well-presented.	
Feedback:					**Total Score:**

Engineering Design Project

The Engineering Design Project (EDP) we use in STEM For Kids programs are meant to mimic, to some extent, the above real-life RFP process and engineering design. Emphasize to children that this is a real process used by engineers when they create technologies.

Explain to participants the stages of the EDP:

- **Ask**: After establishing the goal, we ask questions to understand the goal, the criteria and constraints, and how we will test our solution.
  - Goal - every EDP should have a clear goal. Goals can be laid out as:
    - Simply, build something to apply the concepts being learned.
    - Or, more complex, build / design something to solve a problem. In this case, you can present a problem.
  - Criteria - what are the critical success factors that will determine if the goal has been met? How will these be tested / measured?
  - Constraints - Engineering involves working under constraints. These constraints can be regarding how much money is available, time and people. So, it is important for participants to understand these constraints and work under these conditions.

- **Imagine**: We think about possible solutions by brainstorming ideas, before we choose the best one.

- **Plan**: We draw diagrams for a solution, and decide what materials to use.

- **Create**: Follow your plan, create it, and test it.

- **Improve:** Does your solution work?
  - If so, how can we make it better? If not, how can we improve it?

MODULE 1: Motion Commotion

This module introduces participants to the foundations of mechanical engineering by exploring the relationship between machines, motion, and problem-solving. Through interactive games, discussions, and hands-on building challenges, students learn what machines are, how engineers use science and math to design them, and why motion and force are essential to how things work.

Materials

Materials for Class:
- Laptop/Projector
- Whiteboard
- Classroom Supplies like scissors, crayons, markers, tape/masking tape, pencils, construction/printer paper
- Recycled materials like boxes, bottles, etc.
- Art Supplies like stickers, washy tape, stamps, pipe cleaners, pom poms, cardstock, etc.

Materials for Each Child/Group:
- M&M packets
- Decorations like stickers, gems, glitter, etc.
- Computer per student, optional
- Bag of Mystery Mechanical Objects (1 Each Group)
- Outside Area / Open Area
- Styrofoam Cups (2 Each)
- String (1 Roll)

1.1: M&M - Game of Estimations

Time Required	30 min
Group Sizes	1
Grade	PreK - 5
Materials Needed	

- Laptop / Projector
- Whiteboard/Markers
- M&M Packets
- Paper / Pencil

Learning Objectives
- Understand that a machine is an apparatus using mechanical power and having several parts that work together to perform a specific task.
- Understand that engineers are people who use science and math to make technologies that solve problems.
- Understand that mechanical engineers are a special kind of engineer that makes machines and figures out how something will move to do work.

Tell the participants that in this program (mechanical engineering) we will focus on 2 M's: M&M: *Motion & Machines.*

Machines: <u>Watch the following videos: "The Great Robogator Race," "7 Minutes of Terror – Mars Curiosity Rover," "Mercedes Benz Factory," "Oasis Cruise Ship," "Airbus 380," "Crawler Transporter," "World's Biggest Machines," and "Bugatti Veyron" videos in the STEM For Kids Digital Library.</u>

Explain how each machine uses motion to complete some task.

In between each video, ask participants to identify the task and the motion. *Example: A car uses forward motion to travel.*

Engineers: Ask participants who they think made these machines. Listen to answers before explaining that engineers design and make such machines.

- Discuss engineers with participants, asking questions to gauge their understanding of the profession. Finally explain that engineers are people who use science and math to make technologies that solve problems.

Mechanical engineers are a special kind of engineers that make machines and that they figure out how something will move to do work. Mechanical engineers deal with our two M's a lot, which we will discuss throughout the camp. For now let's focus on another type of M&M.

M&M's: Give each participant a party-sized bag of M&M's® and tell them not to open the bag yet. Complete the following:

- Ask them to estimate (guess) how many M&M's® are in the bag, without opening it. *Note their estimations on the white board.*
- Ask about strategies they used to estimate.
- Give each participant a tissue paper and tell them they can open the bags but not eat any candy yet.
- Have them count the M&Ms®. *Note their actual counts against the estimates and how people over estimated or under estimated.*
- Ask them when estimating like this might be useful. Save time and effort in getting to a close enough answer like: *How many people are in a room, about how much total you will pay for various items purchased.*
- Participants can now eat their candies. *Remind them of our two M's.*

Extension: After the participants have estimated the amount of M&Ms in the pack, you should note them on the white board or the excel file. Have the participants count the actual number of M&Ms, and write the numbers on the white board or excel file.

Then, you can graph the estimated vs. the actual in a bar graph or line graph to see the comparisons. You can either do this as a group or individually.

1.2: Mechanical Mysteries

Time Required	30 min
Group Sizes	2 - 3
Grade	PreK - 5
Materials Needed	

- Laptop / Projector
- Whiteboard/Markers
- Bag of Mystery Mechanical Objects
- Paper / Pencil

Learning Objectives
- Understand that mechanical engineers look at the properties, function, and reason of a technology.
- Understand that we do an action that makes something move to do a task.
- Understand how to collaborate with a team and communicate results to a large group.

Say engineers design and make many different kinds of machines. Engineers are people who use science and math to make technologies that solve problems.

Mechanical engineers are a special kind of engineers who make machines; they figure out how something will move to do a work. Let's think like mechanical engineers. Since we are just beginning ... Let's start with some really simple technologies.

Have a "mystery brown bag" with everyday technologies like scissors, hole punch, glue stick, binder clip, hair clip, and other similar items which need something to be moved to get the resulting action.

Take one prop from the mysteries kit and do a group demo of how to work through the sheet. Example:
- Scissors
  - Made up of plastic and metal (Answers Q3)
  - It cuts paper (Answers Q2/Q4)
  - Move the back handles away and together (Answers Q5)
  - When handles move away, the blades open; when handles come together, blades close making a cut (Answers Q5)

- Binder clip
  - Made up of plastic and metal (Answers Q3)
  - Keeps piles of papers together (Answers Q2/Q4)

14

- Move the metal parts together, clip opens. Release the metal part, clip closes. (Answers Q5)

Note to Coach: The key is for participants to understand that we do something (an action) that makes something move to do the task.

Then split participants into groups of 3 -4.

- Give each group one worksheet

- Participants will work together in their teams for this activity.

- Tell them that when working in teams, it is best to assign responsibilities so everyone can focus to get the activity complete.

- Describe the roles within each group:

  o Writer: the person who will write on the worksheet

  o Leader: the person who will lead the discussion so all work is done

  o Presenter: the person who will tell everyone / present the team's responses to the class.

  o Time keeper: the person who makes sure that discussion and writing of all the responses is completed on time

- Tell each team to think about who will do what. If a team has 3 members, combine Leader and Time Keeper roles.

- Have the writer write each participant's name against the assigned roles in the worksheet.

- Have each team think of a team name. Writer writes the team name on the sheet along with the date

- Give each team one "mystery" item to think about.

- Allocate 5-8 minutes for the team to work on the rest of the worksheet (more time if needed for younger kids).

- Set the timer up on display so everyone can see or set a timer using a phone app.

- Encourage team discussion and exchange of ideas.

- When time is up, check to see if all teams are done; give extra few minutes to complete as needed.

- Have the presenter from each team come to the front of the room and present their team's work.

- Some participants may feel intimidated to come to the front, allowing them to stand and speak from their seat.

- Encourage them to speak.

Mechanical Mystery

Who will do what?

Writer: _____

Leader: _____

Presenter: _____

Time Keeper: _____

1. Our Mechanical technology is _____

2. What does it do? _____

    _____

    _____

3. What is it made of? _____

    _____

4. Why does it exist? _____

    _____

    _____

5. What do you have to do to make it work? _____

    _____

    _____

1.3: Game of Statues

Time Required	15-20 min
Group Sizes	1
Grade	PreK - 5
Materials Needed	
• Outside Area / Open Area	

Learning Objectives
- Understand that motion is a large part of our lives, and it is everywhere!
- Understand that there are scientific laws for motion because it is everywhere.

Play a game of statues with the participants, *which is a slight variation of red light, green light:*
- The instructor is the curator. Participants are statues.
- The curator stands on one side of the room and participants on the other.
- Participants have to tag the curator. But they can only move when the curator's back is to them. When the curator is facing them, participants have to be statues (freeze in position.)
- If they move, they are sent back to the starting position.

Modification: Have the participants stay in one spot in the classroom and run in place when the curator looks away and freezes when the curator turns back and looks at them.

Play the real game 1-3 times. Then in the last play the curator keeps looking at the statues forcing them to stay as statues.
- Keep looking at the statues for about 1 minute, observe participants' reaction (some may start to fidget, express difficulty holding on to their positions).
- Tell them you are doing an experiment and know that this might be getting uncomfortable for them. How long can they stay frozen?

After a few moments of uncomfortable statue positions, "unfreeze" the participants and have them go back to their seats. Ask:
- How long could you stay frozen in a place? How hard was it?
- We keep moving all day long, yet we hardly ever notice it until we have to stop.
- Motion is a part of our lives. It is everywhere!
- Look around – cars, people, birds, insects, leaves swaying, etc.
- Because it is everywhere there are scientific laws of motion.

1.4: Grab-I-Nator™

Time Required	30 min
Group Sizes	1
Grade	PreK - 2
Materials Needed	

- 2 Styrofoam Cups
- String
- Tape
- Scissors
- Stickers/Markers
- Pencil

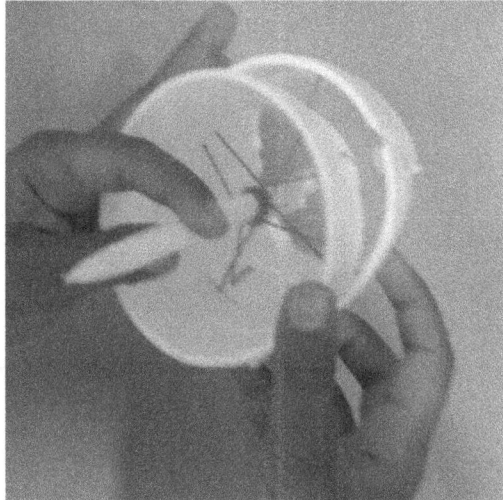

Learning Objectives

- Understand that technologies can be born through even the simplest of motion
- Understand how mechanical engineers use materials around them to design machines.
- Understand how to build and test the Grab-I-Nator™.

When the US space agency, NASA was trying to figure out a way to fix the Hubble Telescope up in space, they had to devise a contraption that could grab onto things. In space, because there is no gravity, things float away.

The story goes that an engineer assigned to design the contraption was sitting in a cafeteria. He ended up creating a simple contraption that would grab things with a simple twisting motion.

Show participants the sample and grab a volunteer's finger in it! Tell participants that we will make our own contraption … Make the contraption … The Grab-Inator™!

Note to Coach: Make the Grab-Inator™ before doing this activity with the participants.

Note to Coach: You can do this activity step-by-step or as an EDP. Suggestion is to use the step-by-step for younger participants and the EDP for older participants with a goal in mind.

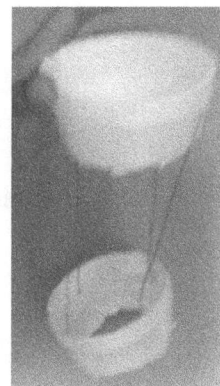

Steps:

- Take 2 cups, cut off the bottoms.
- Take the 4 pieces of 4-6" strings. Tape one end of each string on the outside and top of one cup.
- Tape the other ends to the bottom inside of the other cup.

19

Encourage participants to color their Grab-Inators™!

The contraption is now ready.

To use, with strings straight (not twisted) as shown in the first picture, bring the cups together as if piling one on top of the other.

Ask a volunteer to place a finger or a pen inside the empty space within the cups. Twist the top cup until the strings wind-up to trap the finger/pen. Shown in the 2nd picture.

Encourage participants to color & personalize their Grab – I-Nators™!

1.5: Mechanical Inventions

Time Required	20 min
Group Sizes	1
Grade	PreK - 5
Materials Needed	
• Whiteboard/Markers • Laptop/Projector	

Learning Objectives
- Understand that engineers find out what makes a real-life machine work and the properties of the machine.

In this activity, participants will explore different real-life machines.

Start with discussing a few examples of common mechanical inventions:

- Robot Vacuum Cleaner
- Train
- Bicycle
- Boat
- Car
- Construction Machine

- Helicopter
- Forklift
- Lawn Mower
- Clock
- Blender
- Washing Machine

Bring more engagement by showing participants some grand machines that are the best in their machine type:

- Airbus 380 – biggest passenger air plane
- Mars Rover – world's smartest machine
- Oasis Cruise Ship – biggest passenger cruise ship
- The Crawler Transporter – mammoth machine used to carry space shuttles to the launch site
- Bugatti Veyron – one of the fastest road cars in the world

Show participants videos on various machines on the STEM For Kids Digital Library to get them thinking. Take participants' ideas about other great machines and look at some photos to discuss.

Extension - Presentation:

Allow participants to create a presentation to showcase a technology of their choice. The presentation can be a slide show, poster, animation, video, book, etc.

For younger participants, encourage them to pick one from the list to research and present. For advanced participants, let them pick one of their own.

As each participant presents their selected invention, encourage others to make notes about what they learned about the invention being presented.

1.6: Invention History

Time Required	20 min
Group Sizes	1
Grade	PreK - 2
Materials Needed	

- Whiteboard/Markers
- Laptop/Projector
- Pencil

Learning Objectives

- Understand who Da Vinci was in regards to mechanical engineering through reading comprehension.
- Understand that Da Vinci was an inventor that applied the laws of physics behind mechanical engineering to his machines.

Have participants turn to the Da Vinci Story in their workbook, read the story quietly and respond to the questions.

Give them about 15 minutes.

Then discuss the responses as a group.

The Da Vinci Story

Leonardo Da Vinci is responsible for many mechanical inventions. He dabbled in many areas of science and art with body proportions and the mechanical aspects of nature. The sketches of the human body and paintings we all love were only a side hobby for money when he was not at work with his true job. His true job was military engineering.

Many military engineers of the time were in competition with each other on who could be the primary engineer for certain families in the Italian prestige. Many engineers published military weaponry books, hoping for a family to see their sketches and understand the level of expertise in engineering they held. Da Vinci was not much different from these other engineers. However, he held a personal journal that detailed other inventions that were for fun, not for a job.

One of those inventions is a special type of car. This car can be classified as the first self-propelled vehicle and the first programmable machine in history. Da Vinci's cart was essentially a box-shaped wagon supported by three wheels. Many considered this invention to be the first robot. This cart contained a primitive auto-pilot steering system. The cart also contained a "guide wheel" that pegs were inserted into. The pegs were placed into small holes to tell the wheels of the car to turn at certain points.

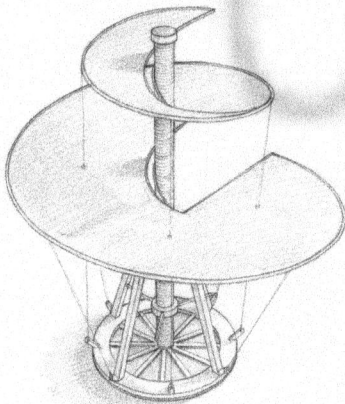

Da Vinci's second invention was a helicopter. He most likely developed the idea for this invention by observing Maple Tree seeds, which spin as they fall to the ground. This invention measures 15 feet in diameter and was made of linen, reed, and wires.

There are many other inventions that Da Vinci sketched out that have a presence in modern engineering. He had to first understand the laws and physics behind mechanical engineering before designing his own inventions. In a way, he used a kit of knowledge to form his inventions.

What is Da Vinci famous for?

_____

_____

_____

How was Da Vinci different from **other** engineers of his era?

_____

_____

_____

How was Da Vinci similar to other engineers of his era?

_____

_____

_____

Describe one of Da Vinci's inventions.

_____

_____

_____

_____

_____

1.7: My Machine EDP

Time Required	45 min
Group Sizes	1 - 2
Grade	PreK - 5
Materials Needed	

- Whiteboard/Markers
- Laptop/Projector
- Classroom Supplies like scissors, crayons, markers, tape/masking tape, pencils, construction/printer paper
- Recycled materials like boxes, bottles, etc.
- Art Supplies like stickers, washy tape, stamps, pipe cleaners, pom poms, cardstock, etc.
- Box of Connected Blocks like Legos

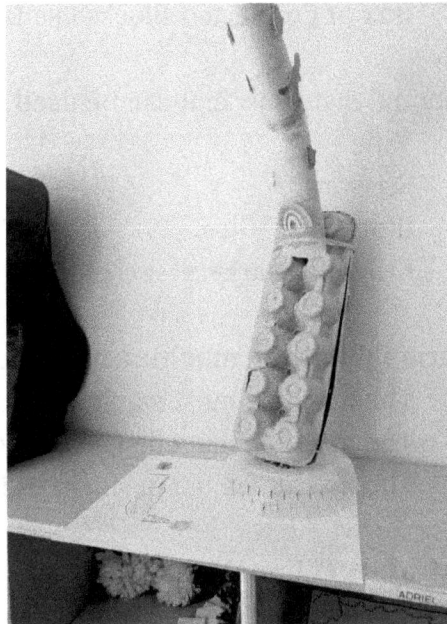

Learning Objectives
- Understand that force is applied to change stable positions.
- Understand that objects can have multiple stable shapes.

Participants will design, build, test, and improve a machine of their choosing using common and recycled materials. Machines may include (but are not limited to) a robot cat, vacuum cleaner, clock, camera, or an original invention. The focus is on understanding how machines work, how motion is created, and how engineers design within criteria and constraints.

Goal:
Guide participants to define an acceptable goal for their machine by thinking about what their machine will do once built.

Sample Goal Statement:
Build a machine that performs a specific task using motion and stays together when tested.

Ask / Imagine:
Have participants ask questions about the project. Explain that engineers often work with limited supplies, so planning is important.

Materials that can be used in this project:
- Classroom Supplies like scissors, crayons, markers, tape/masking tape, pencils, construction/printer paper

- Recycled materials like boxes, bottles, etc.
- Art Supplies like stickers, washy tape, stamps, pipe cleaners, pom poms, cardstock, etc.
- Box of Connected Blocks like Legos

Additional materials that can be used and not part of the design:
- Tape
- Scissors
- Glue dots / Glue
- Crayons, markers, stickers

Criteria (What the machine must do):
- The machine must stay together on its own
- The machine must be free-standing
- The machine must perform its intended task (movement, spinning, lifting, etc.)

Constraints (Limits):
- Use only the materials provided
- Time is limited

Plan:

Distribute the "My Engineering Design Process" worksheet. Have participants draw one possible design for their machine.

Review the available materials together. For each material, ask:
- What does this material look like?
- How does it feel?
- Is it strong, flexible, smooth, rough?
- How could this material be used in a machine?

Encourage participants to think through:
- What parts does their machine need?
  - A body or frame
  - Moving parts (wheels, axles, arms, flaps, etc.)
  - Connections that hold parts together

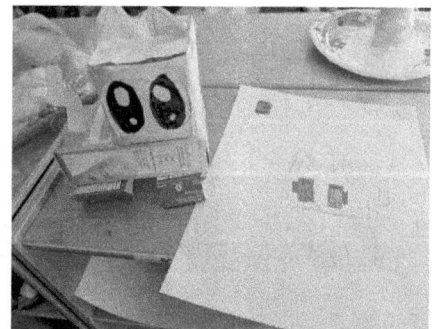

Have participants label: Materials they plan to use; Where each material will go; How much of each material they will need.

Once plans are complete, participants must get teacher approval before building. Ask clarifying questions to ensure their design is realistic and meets criteria. Place a sticker or stamp of approval on their plan and let them know they can begin building.

Build:
Participants begin constructing their machines. Support them as needed but allow creativity and experimentation to lead.

Note to Coach: Younger participants may each build one simple machine. Teams may build one machine per participant or collaborate on variations. Encourage students to test early and often. Allow redesigns after initial testing.

Test:
Have participants test whether their machine:
- Performs its intended task
- Moves as expected (push, pull, spin, roll, lift, etc.)
- Stays together during use

Ask reflection questions:
- What are you using to make it work?
- What parts are moving?
- What happens if you add more weight or change the motion?

Improve:
Allow participants to:
- Change materials
- Strengthen weak points
- Adjust moving parts
- Improve stability or motion

Emphasize that failure is part of engineering and improvement makes designs better.

Communication:
Each participant presents their machine to the group and explains:
- What their machine does
- How it moves
- What materials they used
- What worked well
- What they would improve next time

Note to Coach: Always highlight strengths in every machine and invite peer compliments to build confidence and communication skills.

My Engineering Design Process

Did it work?
YES: How can it be better?
NO: How can we fix it?

What do we have to work with and
what do we want it to do?

Improve

Ask

The Goal:

DO NOT COPY

What have we
learned to
complete this
challenge?

Create

Imagine

Build it!

Plan

Draw out a few ideas on how to
complete this challenge:

My Engineering Design Plan

Material	Properties	How could you use it in your design?

Draw a possible solution:

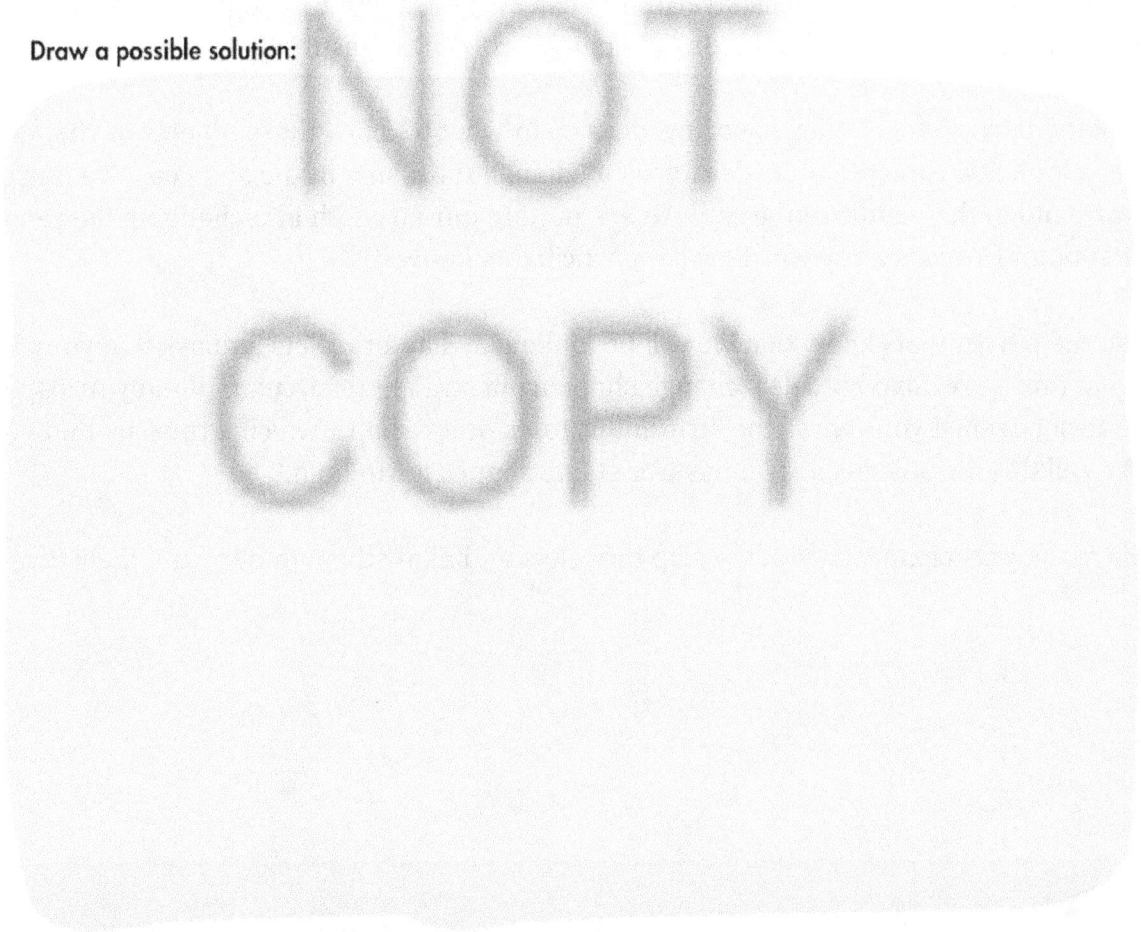

1.8: Motion Slap Bracelets

Time Required	20 min
Group Sizes	1
Grade	PreK - 2
Materials Needed	

- Whiteboard/Markers
- Laptop/Projector
- Slap Bracelets

Learning Objectives
- Understand that force is applied to change stable positions.
- Understand that objects can have multiple stable shapes.

Have the participants think about objects that appear to look one way but can change into another shape or feel. What do they change from and to? Examples can be soda can (comes in a cylinder shape but can be crushed through the middle to form another shape), a tape measure (normally pulled out straight but can curve and bend) and paper clips (comes in regular spiral shape but can be pulled apart). Show the measuring tape example.

Ask the participants if they have any ideas as to what to allow these objects to change shape. Let's look at a soda can. In order for us to change the shape of the soda can, we must squeeze our hand in the middle of the can. We are putting our strength into changing the can shape at that point (force is a key word here if participants know it).

Let the participants know that we will be looking at slap bracelets and ask if anyone knows what those are. Slap bracelets change shape from straight to circular. When you slap the bracelet against your wrist, the strip snaps to its other shape, which wraps around your wrist. We call this bistable because it has two stable shapes it can hold.

Have the participants try out the slap bracelets and allow them to decorate their own.

1.9: Preparing for the Future: AI Integration & Recap

Time Required	20 min
Group Sizes	1 - 2
Grade	PreK - 5

Learning Objectives

- Explore age-appropriate AI & machine learning to enhance understanding of motion & machines.

Here is a curated list of age-appropriate Artificial Intelligence (AI) / Machine Learning (ML) extensions that naturally build on Module 1 Mechanical Engineering lessons. These are designed to be optional enhancements, scalable from PreK through Grade 5, and aligned with your focus on motion, machines, data, and design thinking.

1.1 M&M - Game of Estimations

- Chatbot Estimation Coach (PreK–5):
  - Use a simple classroom chatbot (teacher-guided) to ask:
  - "What strategies can I use to make a good estimate?"
  - "Was my estimate high or low compared to others?"
  - The chatbot models reasoning, not answers.

- Prediction vs Reality AI Discussion (Grades 3–5):
  - Introduce AI as a "prediction helper" and compare:
    - Human estimates vs. computer-generated averages
    - Discuss how AI learns from data but doesn't guess like humans

- Graphing with AI Tools (Grades 2–5):
  - Input estimates and actual counts into a spreadsheet or chart-making tool.
    - Bar graph: Estimate vs Actual
    - Line graph: Difference between estimate and count

- Pattern Recognition (Grades 4–5):
  - Ask: "Did students who shook the bag estimate higher?"
  - Discuss how ML looks for patterns in data like this.

1.2 Mechanical Mysteries

- AI Role-Play: Mechanical Engineer (Grades 3–5):
  - Chatbot pretends to be a mechanical engineer asking:
    - "What part moves?"
    - "What action causes motion?"

- Simple Classification Game:
  - Students sort objects into categories:
    - Push machines
    - Pull machines
    - Twist machines
  - The teacher explains how ML learns by sorting examples the same way.

1.3 Game of Statues

- Motion-Detecting Animation (Grades K–5):
  - Use a simple webcam or animation to show how computers detect motion vs stillness.
    - Recommended: https://teachablemachine.withgoogle.com/
  - Connect to:
    - "How does AI know when we're moving?"

- Human vs Computer Detection:
  - Compare how humans notice movement vs how AI looks for pixel changes.

1.4 Grab-Inator™

- Design Improvement Chatbot:
  - Students ask:
    - "How can I make my Grab-I-Nator grab better?"
    - "What happens if I twist faster?"

- Trial Data Collection (Grades 2–5):
  - Track:
    - Number of twists
    - Object grabbed
    - Success/failure
  - Show how ML learns from repeated tests.

1.5 Mechanical Inventions

- AI Research Assistant (Grades 3–5):
  - Students ask:
    - "What problem does a washing machine solve?"
    - "What parts move in a clock?"

- AI-Generated Diagrams (Teacher-led):
  - Show simplified AI images of machines and identify moving parts.

1.6 Invention History with Da Vinci

- Chat with "Leonardo" (Teacher-guided):
  - AI role-plays Leonardo da Vinci answering simple questions:
    - "Why did you design machines?"
    - "How did motion help your inventions?"

- Timeline Pattern Recognition
  - Compare old inventions to modern machines - how designs evolve over time.

1.7 My Machine EDP

- AI Brainstorming Partner:
  - Students ask:
    - "What kind of machine could I build?"
    - "What moves in my machine?"

- AI Reflection Prompts:
  - After testing:
    - "What worked?"
    - "What should I change?"

1.8 Motion Slap Bracelets

- AI Shape-Change Explainer:
  - Chatbot explains bistable objects using age-appropriate language.

- Slow-Motion AI Video (Teacher-led):
  - Show how AI can slow down motion to observe shape changes.
    - Recommended: Microsoft ClipChamp

Module 2: Laziness & Motion

This module introduces Newton's three laws of motion with a focused exploration of the first law - inertia. Through hands-on experiments and build challenges, students investigate how objects at rest and in motion behave, observe inertia in real-world scenarios, and connect these concepts to safety features like seatbelts.

Materials

Materials for Class:
- Laptop/Projector
- Whiteboard/Markers
- Classroom Supplies like scissors, crayons, markers, tape/masking tape, pencils, construction/printer paper
- Recycled materials like boxes, bottles, etc.
- Art Supplies like stickers, washy tape, stamps, pipe cleaners, pom poms, cardstock, etc.
- Box of Connected Blocks like Legos

Materials for Each Child/Group:
- Toy Person / Animal (1 Each)
- Rubber Bands
- Small Cups (1 Each)
- Popsicle Sticks
- Small Ball (1 Each Group)
- Basket / Bowl (1 Each Group)
- Cups (9 Each Group)
- Index Card (1 Each)
- Coin (1 Each)
- Table

2.1: Newton and the Laws of Motion

Time Required	15 min
Group Sizes	1
Grade	PreK - 5
Materials Needed	

- Whiteboard/Markers
- Laptop/Projector

Learning Objectives
- Understand that there are three laws of motion: Inertia, Force, and Action-Reaction.
- Understand that Sir Isaac Newton discovered gravity and the three laws of motion.

Story Time - Tell participants a story:
There was once a child born to a farmer in England more than 300 years ago. He worked through schools waiting tables and grew up to be a great scientist who is remembered for his work in many areas. Once, while he was lying under an apple tree, an apple fell on this head.

Ask participants, "What would you do?" Take participants' responses. What did the man do? He wondered why the apple fell down and not up! He thought long and hard and began to experiment until he finally discovered a mysterious

33

force that we know today as ***gravity***! The scientist then also made amazing discoveries about motion that we rely upon today.

Ask participants if they can guess the scientist's name. Tell them he was *Sir Isaac Newton.* <u>Watch the "Gravity for kids" video on the SFK Sites.</u>

Ask participants to think back to the game of statues where we saw that motion was everywhere, and we hardly noticed it. Sir Isaac Newton noticed motion and tried to understand it. To do this, he made 3 laws of motion.

Note for Coach: Emphasize Newton's laws of motion in the first flight. Newton's Laws are three physical laws that together laid the foundation for classical mechanics. They describe the relationship between a body and the force acting upon it, and its motion in response to said forces. They have been expressed in several different ways over nearly three centuries, and can be summarized as follows:

- **First law**: An object at rest remains at rest unless acted upon by a force. An object in motion remains in motion, and at a constant velocity, unless acted upon by a force.

- **Second law**: The acceleration of a body is directly proportional to, and in the same direction as, the net force acting on the body, and inversely proportional to its mass. Thus, $\mathbf{F} = m\mathbf{a}$, where $\mathbf{F}$ is the net force acting on the object, m is the mass of the object and $\mathbf{a}$ is the acceleration of the object.

- **Third law**: When one body exerts a force on a second body, the second body simultaneously exerts a force equal in magnitude and opposite in direction to that of the first body.

Source: Newton's Laws of Motions on Wikipedia

Discuss: Avoid formulas in your discussion of the laws and use simplistic terms when describing the laws to participants. Below is a description in very simple terms:
Newton's Three Laws of Motion
1.   Everything is lazy, doesn't move unless a force is applied – Inertia or Laziness
2.   More force is needed to move heavier objects or to go farther
3.   For every action, there is an equal and opposite reaction

<u>Watch "The Laws of Motion and Bicycles" video on the STEM For Kids Digital Library.</u>

2.2: Law 1 - Coin Flip

Time Required	10 min
Group Sizes	1
Grade	PreK - 5
Materials Needed	

- Index Card
- Coin
- Table

Learning Objectives
- Understand that a body at rest wants to stay at rest and a body in motion wants to stay in motion, which is called inertia.
- Understand that a coin experiences inertia by staying in place when an index card is pulled fast from underneath it.
- Understand that a coin experiences inertia by moving with an index card when it is pulled slowly.

Put a coin on an index card at the corner of a table. Ask participants to predict what will happen if we flick the card? *Listen to answers and take a poll, "Who thinks it will fall down?" Have them explain their thoughts.*
- Flick the card and observe what happens.
- If the card is flicked fast enough, as the card moves underneath, the coin tries to stay put due to *inertia*.
- If the card is pulled slowly, there is enough time for the motion to travel from the card to the coin and the coin moves with the card.

Let the participants try with an index card and a penny, then make it challenging by consolidating coins. Add an extra layer of difficulty by having them make shapes with their coins and attempting to maintain their shapes while flicking the card. *Examples: tower of coins, corners of an imaginary square.*

First Law of Motion Comprehension
Everybody wants (the pen and coin) to keep doing what they are doing, and this is called the first law of motion - *inertia*. If the participants cannot remember the word inertia well, substitute the word for "laziness":
- A body at rest wants to stay at rest. Ask participants, do you feel inertia when your morning alarm goes off?
- A body in motion wants to stay in motion. Ask participants, do you feel inertia when you are playing your favorite game?

A force (push or pull) is needed to move or stop something.

35

2.3: Cup Tower Challenge

Time Required	30 min
Group Sizes	1 - 2
Grade	PreK - 5
Materials Needed	

- Paper
- Cups

Learning Objectives

- Understand that cups in a tower formation experience inertia by falling into one another when a piece of paper is pulled quickly from under the cups.
- Understand how to design and build the cup tower challenge.

In the front of the room, stack 2 towers to show the participants. Have them make each tower at their group table and try to complete the challenge.

The challenge is to pull the piece of papers out of the tower without the tower falling. Explain that they will need to pull the paper swiftly and quickly.

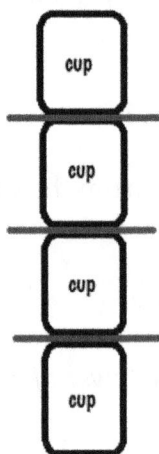

Tower 1: Place one cup face down on the table. Put a piece of printer paper on top of the cup. Place another cup face down on top of the printer paper. Put another piece of printer paper on top of the exposed cup. Do this two more times.

Tower 2: Begin by placing three cups upside down next to each other on a table. Place a piece of printer paper on top of each cup on the ends. You may have some of the paper on the middle cup. Place two cups on top of the printer paper face down. Put a piece of printer paper in the middle of the two cups on top. Complete tower 1 on top of the above base.

Tower 3: Have the participants create their own tower to challenge other teams. Remember to have them place a piece of paper between the cups for the challenge.

Note to Coach: You can use blocks instead of cups.

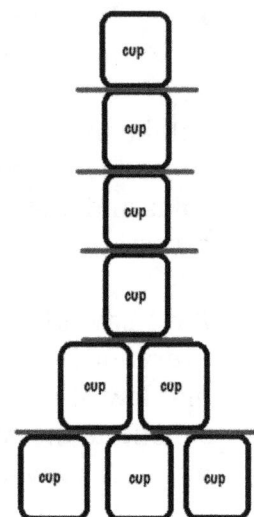

2.4: The Ball Drop Sprint

Time Required	30 min
Group Sizes	4 - 6
Grade	PreK - 5
Materials Needed	

- Small Ball
- Basket / Bowl
- Masking Tape

Start   Target

Learning Objectives

- Understand that an object in motion wants to stay in motion, even if it is experiencing gravity (falling down.)
- Understand that a body in motion will continue in motion in a straight line unless acted upon by an outside force.

Procedure: You will need to complete this activity in an open area.

1) Place a target about 20 – 30 feet away from a starting line. Mark the starting line with chalk or tape.

2) Hold one participant hold the ball; their elbow should be on their side as they run and drop the ball. Do not throw the ball. Remember to drop the ball and not throw it, otherwise you will change the intent of the experiment.

3) Have three students stand alongside (but slightly back from) the running path to act as observers. One should stand before the target, one at the target, and one just after the target. Their objective is to determine exactly where the runner released the ball and where the ball strikes the ground.

4) Ask the runner to sprint toward the target as fast as she or he can and try to drop the ball so that it lands on the target.

5) Next, have the observers make a diagram of where the ball was released and where it landed. Repeat the experiment with another set of 4 participants. You can have each participant take a turn being a runner.

6) Predict what would happen if a student ran at a slower speed.

7) Repeat Steps 4-5, using a different runner sprinting at a slower speed.

8) Use the information in the previous trials to predict what would happen at a walking speed.

9) For the last trial, ask a student to walk toward the target and repeat Steps 4-5.

10) Summarize the conclusions based on the speed of each runner, the location of each ball's release, and the exact point where each ball landed.

Inertia – A Body in Motion

When running, students will miss the target when the ball is dropped directly over it. The ball needs to be dropped before the target is actually reached. As the ball drops, its horizontal motion remains unchanged because there is no force in that direction. Newton's First Law applies to horizontal motion.

You might have your students start this activity by rolling (or pushing) the ball on the floor, and observing its constant velocity once they let go of it. This is another application of Newton's First Law of Motion: A body in motion will continue in motion in a straight line unless acted upon by an outside force. In this case, the motion is that of the runner, and gravity is the outside force.

Possible Extensions:

- Try the experiment again using a smaller target.

- If you have access to a digital camera, enhance the activity by filming each runner (with a wide angle) and the path of each drop. Slow motion of the video will allow your class to analyze the trajectories.

Inertia Extension

Observe the effect of inertia when you ride back home and think about why you wear a seat belt:

- When the car starts moving, our body has been at rest and wants to stay as such, so we feel a slight jerk to the back.

- When the car is moving, our bodies are in forward motion with the car.

- When the car brakes, our body shows inertia, it wants to stay in forward motion so we jerk forward.

- In a sudden stop (like in an accident), without a seatbelt, a person can be thrown forward getting hurt more severely than they would with a seatbelt.

2.5: Law 1 - Blocks Car

Time Required	45 min
Group Sizes	1 - 3
Grade	PreK - 5
Materials Needed	

- Lego-Type Blocks (Including Wheels)
- Toy Person / Animal
- Pipe Cleaners
- Rubber Bands
- Small Cups
- Popsicle Sticks
- Paper

Learning Objectives
- Understand that an object will keep moving even if the object it is riding on stops.
- Understand that seatbelts are available to stop us from moving forward due to inertia when a car stops.

Explain to the participants that we will be building a blocks car, using connecting blocks such as lego blocks. Ask if they have any ideas on what this car will do. Let the participants know that we will be investigating inertia by experimenting if a seat belt is needed to be worn in a car. Ask the participants what is their favorite car or what car their parents drive.

What we will be building is a car that will move forward. We will be attaching a basket to the car and placing an object inside. We will be finding out what happens when the car suddenly stops.

Have the participants build the model of the lego car. Above shows a lego car that you can make. However, there are many different models and designs that can occur.

Goal:
Build a car that can move forward and safely carry a passenger, then investigate what happens when the car suddenly stops to explore Newton's First Law of Motion (Inertia).

Materials to be used:
- LEGO or connecting blocks
- LEGO wheels and axles (or block-based wheel pieces)
- Small basket or container (built from blocks or classroom materials)
- Toy person or small object (passenger)

Explain to participants that engineers work with limited materials, so they must plan carefully to make sure their car can move, stop, and hold a passenger safely.

Criteria:
- The car must move forward when pushed.
- The car must be free-standing and stay together during testing.
- The car must include a basket or holder for a passenger.
- The passenger must fit inside the basket without being held by hands.

Constraints:
- Use only the provided LEGO or connecting block materials.
- The car must be moved by pushing - no motors or ramps unless provided.
- The passenger may not be taped or glued into place.

Compare results between different car designs and discuss which worked best and why. After they are done building, have them think through how the car will begin moving. They will need to push the car in order to get it to move.

Prompt the participants to test their cars and make sure they move first. Once they have tested their cars, have the participants attach the basket that they have created to their cars. Hand them a toy person to place in the basket. Have the participants observe what happens when the car suddenly stops with the person in the basket. How does this connect to the first law of motion?

Test: Place the participants into teams of 2. Have one participant in each team line up side by side on a wall. Have the cars at the ready position on the floor. Let the participants know that, on the count of 3, they will push their car forward.

Have the other participant at the other end of the room, watching the car as it is pushed to them. Let them know to look at the army man in the basket to see what happens.

Ask the participants if they have ever been in their parent's car and they suddenly stop. What did the participants do? They moved forward even though the car did not! This is because when the car is in motion, everything in the car wants to stay in motion. However, when the car suddenly stops, everything in the car wants to continue moving forward, causing you to move forward!

How can we eliminate ourselves from moving forward when the car suddenly stops? Have the participants design a seatbelt for their army man to keep him in place.

Test: Have the participants about 2-3 feet away from a wall. Have them push the car towards the wall. Prompt the other participant to see what happens to the army man with a seat belt when the car hits the wall.

My Engineering Design Process

Did it work?
YES: How can it be better?
NO: How can we fix it?

What do we have to work with and what do we want it to do?

Improve

Ask

The Goal:

What have we learned to complete this challenge?

Create

Imagine

Build it!

Plan

Draw out a few ideas on how to complete this challenge:

My Engineering Design Plan

Material	Properties	How could you use it in your design?

Draw a possible solution:

2.6: Preparing for the Future: AI Integration & Recap

Time Required	20 min
Group Sizes	1 - 2
Grade	PreK - 5

Learning Objectives

- Explore age-appropriate AI & machine learning to enhance understanding of motion & machines.

Here is a curated list of age-appropriate Artificial Intelligence (AI) / Machine Learning (ML) extensions that naturally build on Module 2 Mechanical Engineering lessons. These are designed to be optional enhancements, scalable from PreK through Grade 5, and aligned with your focus on motion, machines, data, and design thinking.

2.1 Newton and the Laws of Motion	2.2 Law 1 - Coin Flip
<ul><li>Chat with "Newton" (Teacher-Guided) (PreK–5):<ul><li>Use a classroom chatbot role-playing as Sir Isaac Newton to ask:<ul><li>"Why do things fall down?"</li><li>"What makes something start moving?"</li><li>"What happens when something stops?"</li></ul></li><li>The chatbot models curiosity and observation rather than formulas.</li></ul></li><li>AI Story Reflection Prompts (Grades K–5):<ul><li>After the Newton story, students ask:<ul><li>"What question did Newton wonder about?"</li><li>"What would you experiment with?"</li></ul></li><li>Connect to how scientists and AI both start by asking questions.</li></ul></li><li>Law Sorting Game (Grades 1–5):<ul><li>Show motion examples (bike stopping, ball rolling, jumping).</li><li>Students classify each as:<ul><li>Inertia</li><li>Force</li><li>Action–Reaction</li></ul></li><li>Explain that ML learns by sorting examples the same way.</li></ul></li></ul>	<ul><li>Prediction Coach Chatbot (PreK–5):<ul><li>Students ask:<ul><li>"What will happen if I pull the index card under a coin fast?"</li><li>"What if I pull slow?"</li></ul></li><li>The chatbot encourages predictions before testing.</li></ul></li><li>Prediction vs Outcome Charting (Grades 2–5):<ul><li>Record:<ul><li>Pull speed</li><li>Coin behavior</li></ul></li><li>Create a simple bar chart showing results.</li></ul></li><li>Pattern Recognition Discussion (Grades 3–5):<ul><li>Ask:<ul><li>"When did the coin move?"</li><li>"What stayed the same each time?"</li></ul></li><li>Explain that ML looks for patterns in repeated tests.</li></ul></li></ul>

2.3 Cup Tower Challenge
- Design Strategy Chatbot (Grades 1–5):
  - Students ask:
    - "How can I pull the paper without knocking cups over?"
    - "Should I pull fast or slow?"
  - The chatbot reinforces inertia using simple language.

- Trial & Error Data Tracking (Grades 2–5):
  - Track:
    - Tower design
    - Pull speed
    - Success or collapse
  - Create a class chart showing which designs worked best.

- AI Pattern Talk (Grades 4–5):
  - Discuss:
    - "Which tower stayed standing most often?"
    - "What design choices mattered most?"
  - Relate to how ML improves from trial results.

2.4 The Ball Drop Sprint
- AI Prediction Helper (PreK–5):
  - Before the run, students ask:
    - "If I run fast, where will the ball land?"
    - "What if I walk?"
  - Compare predictions to actual outcomes.

- Motion Mapping with AI Tools (Grades 3–5):
  - Use slow-motion video to observe:
    - Release point
    - Landing point
  - Draw motion paths and compare trials.
    - Recommended: https://teachablemachine.withgoogle.com/

- Speed vs Distance Graphing (Grades 2–5):
  - Create a chart showing:
    - Runner speed
    - Where the ball landed
  - Explain how AI uses graphs to learn from motion data.

2.5 Law 1 - Blocks Car
- Engineering Design Chatbot (Grades 1–5):
  - Students ask:
    - "How can I keep my passengers safe?"
    - "What happens if the car stops fast?"
  - The chatbot prompts thinking about inertia and safety.

- Seatbelt Test Data Collection (Grades 2–5):
  - Track:
    - Seatbelt or no seatbelt
    - Passenger stays or moves
    - Speed & Distance Travelled
  - Create a simple comparison chart.

- Safety & AI Discussion (Grades 3–5):
  - Connect:
    - Seatbelts in real cars
    - How engineers test designs
  - Explain how AI helps engineers test many designs quickly and safely.

Module 3: Inertia Fruit Basket EDP

This module challenges participants to apply the Engineering Design Process to design, build, and improve a head-balancing device, deepening their understanding of inertia and balance. Through hands-on testing and iteration, participants explore how forces interact to keep objects stable while meeting specific goals, criteria, and constraints, reinforcing problem-solving, design thinking, and real-world applications of mechanical engineering concepts.

Materials

Materials for Class:
- Laptop/Projector
- Whiteboard/Markers
- Classroom Supplies like scissors, crayons, markers, tape/masking tape, pencils, construction/printer paper
- Recycled materials like boxes, bottles, etc.
- Art Supplies like stickers, washy tape, stamps, pipe cleaners, pom poms, cardstock, etc.
- Box of Connected Blocks like Legos

Materials for Each Child/Group:
- Book (1 Each Group)
- Spoon (1 Each)
- Pom Pom (1 Each)
- Beanbag (or plastic bag filled with rice) (1 Each Group)

3.1: Balancing Tests

Time Required	30 min
Group Sizes	2 - 4
Grade	PreK - 5
Materials Needed	

- Whiteboard/Markers
- Laptop/Projector
- Painters tape
- Book
- Spoon
- Pom Pom
- Beanbag (or plastic bag filled with rice)

Learning Objectives
- Understand that balancing is the act of equal distribution of weight, amount, etc.
- Understand that inertia is happening even when something is balancing, but another force is acting on the object to keep it from continuing to move.

Have the participants think about what balancing means. When have they balanced something? Have they tried balancing themselves?

45

Prompt the participants to stand up. Have them place one foot off the ground and try to balance.

What are some things they have to do to keep their balance? Maybe they need to hold their arms out or move their feet that are on the ground every so often. Ask why they think they need to have their arms out – they need to have the weight be distributed evenly on their body!

Have the participants play the following balancing games. Have them think about the first law of motion and why balancing occurs or why things fall.

Here are some balancing games you can do to emphasize how to balance:

1.   Place a long piece of painters tape on the ground for each team. Explain that they will need to balance on the painter tape as it represents a tight rope. If they get off the tight rope, then that means they have fallen!

       After they have done the tight rope, have them be challenged to balance a book on their head while balancing on the tape! After the book balancing, you can also do a challenge of a spoon with a pom pom on it.

       Note to Coach: You can make it a race by having each team member complete each challenge!

2.   Hand each participant a beanbag (or a plastic bag filled with rice). Explain that they will need to line up in their team at the start line. They will place their beanbag on the top of their foot.

       Participants will need to try to walk like a penguin without dropping their egg to the other side of the room. The first team to complete the challenge wins the race.

3.2: Inertia Fruit Basket EDP

Time Required	45 min
Group Sizes	1 - 2
Grade	PreK - 5

Materials Needed
<ul><li>Whiteboard/Markers</li><li>Laptop/Projector</li><li>Classroom Supplies like scissors, crayons, markers, tape/masking tape, pencils, construction/printer paper</li><li>Recycled materials like boxes, bottles, plates, cups, bowls, etc.</li><li>Art Supplies like stickers, washy tape, stamps, pipe cleaners, pom poms, cardstock, etc.</li><li>Box of Connected Blocks like Legos</li><li>Fake Fruit OR Classroom Helper / Toy</li></ul>

Learning Objectives

- Understand how to engineer and design a contraption that keeps an object on the top of our head by understanding the concept of inertia.
- Understand the application of the engineering design process to certain goals, criteria, and constraints.

For the engineering design process, hand each participant a fake fruit. Explain that we are going to be trying to balance this piece of fruit on our heads. Think about how the first law helps or hinders the fruit when balancing.

First, test how the fruit balances on their head without restraints. Prompt the participants to think about what direction the fruit falls or how it falls. Have the participants line up on one side of the room side by side. Tell them to place their fruit on their head and try to balance it. On the count of 3, have the participants race to the other side of the room while also keeping the fruit on their head. If the fruit falls off, they must stop at that spot and sit down on the floor.

Take a piece of painters tape and mark where each participant's fruit fell off (place name on tape). Explain that we are now going to design and build restraints for our fruit to stay balanced on our head. We want to go past the tape marked with our name each time we do the test and improve.

Goal: Make a restraint for our fruit to balance on our heads out of materials provided:

- Recycled materials like boxes, bottles, plates, cups, bowls, etc.
- Art Supplies like stickers, washy tape, stamps, pipe cleaners, pom poms, string, popsicle sticks, cardstock, construction/printer paper, etc.
- Box of Connected Blocks like Legos
- Fake Fruit OR Classroom Helper / Toy

Materials to help build but will not be used as part of your design.

- Classroom Supplies like scissors, crayons, markers, tape/masking tape, pencils, etc.

Explain when engineers work their supplies are limited, so they have to plan for a small amount of supplies.

Criteria:

- The fruit / toy should not fall off the head.
- The fruit / toy needs to be balanced on the center of the head.
- The fruit / toy must be secured to the contraption.

Constraints

- Use only the materials as specified.

Test

- Place fruit / toy contraption on head and race to the other side of the room.

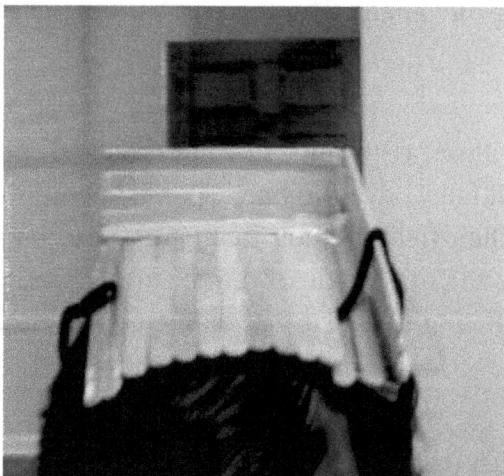

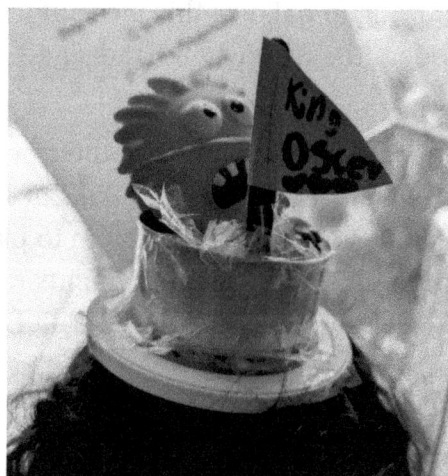

My Engineering Design Process

Did it work?
YES: How can it be better?
NO: How can we fix it?

What do we have to work with and
what do we want it to do?

Improve

Ask

The Goal:

DO NOT COPY

What have we
learned to
complete this
challenge?

Create

Build it!

Imagine

Plan

Draw out a few ideas on how to
complete this challenge:

My Engineering Design Plan

Material	Properties	How could you use it in your design?

Draw a possible solution:

Module 4: May the Forces Be With You

This module focuses on Newton's Second Law of Motion by helping participants explore how forces (pushes and pulls) affect movement. Through hands-on experiments, ramp activities, and building a force pop-up character, students discover how mass, speed, and force change how objects move and apply these concepts to real-world motion.

Materials

Materials for Class:
- Laptop/Projector
- Whiteboard/Markers
- Classroom Supplies like scissors, crayons, markers, tape/masking tape, pencils, construction/printer paper
- Art Supplies like stickers, washy tape, stamps, pipe cleaners, pom poms, cardstock, etc.
- Ruler / Measuring Tape
- Stapler

Materials for Each Child/Group:
- Bucket / Bowl (1 Each Group)
- Ping Pong Ball (1 Each)
- Rubber Ball (1 Each)
- Medium Paper Cups (2 Each)
- Rubber Bands (1 Each)
- Wooden Ramp (1 Each Group)
- Toy Cars (1 Each Group)

4.1: Laws of Motion Recap

Time Required	10 min
Group Sizes	1
Grade	PreK - 5
Materials Needed	

- Whiteboard/Markers
- Laptop/Projector

Learning Objectives
- Understand that there are three laws of motion: Inertia, Force, and Action-Reaction.

Recap the laws of motion. Newton's Laws are three physical laws that together laid the foundation for classical mechanics. They describe the relationship between a body and the force acting upon it, and its motion in response to said forces.

They have been expressed in several different ways over nearly three centuries, and can be summarized as follows:

- **First law**: An object at rest remains at rest unless acted upon by a force. An object in motion remains in motion, and at a constant velocity, unless acted upon by a force.
- **Second law**: The acceleration of a body is directly proportional to, and in the same direction as, the net force acting on the body, and inversely proportional to its mass. Thus, $\mathbf{F} = m\mathbf{a}$, where $\mathbf{F}$ is the net force acting on the object, m is the mass of the object and $\mathbf{a}$ is the acceleration of the object.
- **Third law**: When one body exerts a force on a second body, the second body simultaneously exerts a force equal in magnitude and opposite in direction to that of the first body.

Source: Newton's Laws of Motions on Wikipedia

Discuss: Avoid formulas in your discussion of the laws and use simplistic terms when describing the laws to participants. Below is a description in very simple terms:

Newton's Three Laws of Motion
- Everything is lazy, doesn't move unless a force is applied – Inertia
- More force is needed to move heavier objects or to go farther
- For every action, there is an equal and opposite reaction.

4.2: Law 2 - Explore Forces

Time Required	30 min
Group Sizes	1
Grade	PreK - 2
Materials Needed	

- Whiteboard/Markers
- Laptop/Projector
- Ruler / Measuring Tape
- Bucket / Bowl
- Printer Paper
- Ping Pong Balls
- Rubber Balls

<u>Learning Objectives</u>
- Understand that a force is a push or pull.
- Understand that an object moves by either a push or pull when a force is applied to it through experimentation.
- Understand that heavier objects require more force to get moving.
- Understand how to analyze data by creating graphs and answering critical thinking questions.

Ask participants, what makes things move? Give each participant an index card. Ask them to try different ways to make the card move. Ask participants to share their ideas while you write them on display. Relate all ideas to push or pull forces. (I.e. moving the card with your finger across the table is push)

Have the participants repeat the following statement with arm movements - You will use this mantra throughout the rest of the course as to recap what is a force:

A Force is a PUSH or a PULL.

When you say the word 'push,' push out your hands in front of you. When you say the word 'pull,' pretend to grab rope and pull your hands back towards your body. Do this a few times with the class following along.

Call three volunteers; give each a ping pong ball. Have them **flick** the ball from a marked starting point. [Note: we are using **flick** to simulate an almost constant force]. Tell them we want to know how far the ball went. Ask them, how would we do that?

Take participants' responses. *We need to measure it.*
How will we measure it? *Distance or a length.*
What are the units of measuring distance? *Inches, feet, yard, etc.*

How will you measure and what can we use? *Have someone walk and measure in foot distance.* Discuss advantages and disadvantages of such a measurement. *Non-standard: different people will come up with different results based on their foot size.* Demonstrate this by having a participant measure and then you measure with your feet.

How about a ruler? Discuss advantages and disadvantages. *Especially with longer distances it can get really cumbersome. But it is a standard measure.* How about a Measuring tape? Ask participants, given the distance they rolled, what would be the best tool to measure? *Have the participants decide themselves.*

Measure the distance the ball travels before stopping. Have participants measure so they are engaged in the activity. Use volunteers when you can.

Repeat with other participants flicking the ball. Show participants if someone pushes with a greater force, the ball goes farther. Then have participants repeat the steps with a rubber ball. Ask participants which goes further when applied the same amount of force? *The ping pong ball, because it is lighter.* Explain this is also a part of the second law.

Extension - Grades 2 to 5:

Draw or use Excel to graph the scatter graphs, one for the light push and another for the harder push, to see which causes the greatest distance. You can either draw a graph on the whiteboard or use Excel to do this. Ask questions about which gave us the most distance and if we all used the same force or not (for the distances that may be far outside the normal range of distances).

Forces in Action: Paper Ball Challenge

Watch the "Make a paper ball – follow along" video on the STEM For Kids Digital Library to create a paper ball using origami.

Make sure participants write their name on the ball prior to blowing it up. Have participants experience the forces as they flick and push their ball. Explain our pushing and/or pulling is making the ball move.

Ask them to flick the ball with a lot of force and ask them what happens. *The ball goes further.*

Ball Activities:

Participants can play a basketball game using a bucket, cup or a ring (like hula hoop), while the coach counts up the number of goals for the game. On a new round move the bucket back a few steps and explain this is Newton's Second Law of Motion: With more force, an object can go further.

Note to Coach: Don't let participants color the balls; it will weigh the paper down. Also, be sure to watch the video prior to working with participants, and only use printer paper.

Second Law of Motion Comprehension

Explain to participants that, when they were throwing the ping pong and rubber balls, they were seeing Newton's second law. Ask them to remember which ball went the furthest and why. *The ping pong ball, because it is lighter.* This is also a part of the law; heavier objects need more force to move.

4.3: Force Pop-Up Frog

Time Required	30 min
Group Sizes	1
Grade	PreK - 2
Materials Needed	

- Medium Paper Cups
- Stapler
- Rubber Bands
- Tape
- Scissors
- Art Supplies like stickers, washy tape, stamps, pipe cleaners, pom poms, cardstock, etc.

Learning Objectives
- Understand that a force is a push or a pull and that changing the amount of force changes how an object moves by building and testing a pop-up frog.

Setup (Before Class):
- Cut out frog face templates (or pre-cut shapes for PreK). You can also create a bunny.

- Check rubber bands for safety (no cracks).

- Prepare the bottom cup mechanism for each participant before class.
  - See Step 2 for directions on how to build the mechanism.

- Pre-model one completed pop-up frog to show students.

Introduction:

Say the following: "Today, we are engineers and scientists! We are going to build a pop-up frog. When we push it down and let go, it will POP! We are learning about force. Who remembers—what is a force?" *(Guide answers toward push and pull.)*

Prompt Questions:

- "What happens when you push something?"

- "What happens when you push harder?"

Step-by-Step Build Instructions:

1. Decorate the Frog
   a. Give each student one paper cup (this will be the top) and the frog template.

   b. Have students color and decorate their frog template and paper cup.

   c. Tape or staple the frog template to cup (open end facing down).

   This is a good moment to build excitement... "Your frog is going to jump!"

2. Provide the Base Cup
   a. Give each participant the bottom cup mechanism already pre-built. Use the steps below to build it for each participant.

      i. Place this cup upright on the table (open end facing up).

      ii. Cut two slits on one side of the cup - See photo.

      iii. Fold up the cut slits on the cup - See photo.

      iv. Cut two slits on the opposite side of the cup directly across from the original cut slits.

      v. Fold up the cut slits on the other side of the cup.

      vi. Take a rubber band, connect to one of the cut slits and staple the cut slit to the cup with the fold upwards - See photo.

      vii. Twist the rubber band once, stretch it across the opening of the base cup, and connect to the other cut slits. Staple the cut slit to the cup with the fold upwards. The rubber band should not be able to come off the cup.

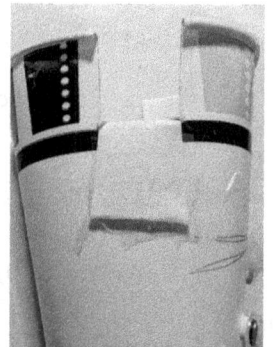

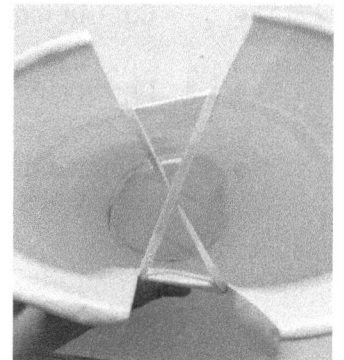

   Explain to the participants when you hand the cup mechanism: "This cup will help our frog pop up and down. This rubber band is like a spring. When we push it down, it wants to go back up."

3. Connect the Frog
   a. Place the decorated cup upside down on top of the base cup mechanism.
   b. Gently push the top cup down until it presses against the rubber band.
   c. Let it go and see what happens!

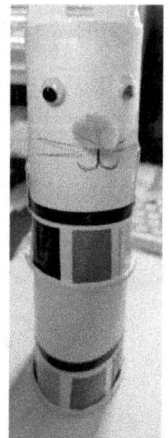

Tests:

Have participants spread out and test their pop-up frogs. Say, "Let's be scientists. Watch what happens when you use different pushes."

- Soft Push Test
    - Say, "Push your frog down gently. What happens?"

- Strong Push Test
    - Say, "Now push harder. What happened this time?"

- Repeat Test
    - Say, "Does it pop the same way every time?"

Science Talk: Connecting to Force

Gather students in a circle with their characters. Ask These Questions:

- "What force did you use to make it move?"
  → A push

- "What happened when you pushed harder?"
  → It popped higher / faster

- "What happened when you pushed softer?"
  → It didn't pop as high

Say to the group: "When we push, we use force. A bigger push makes a bigger movement. That's how force works!"

Encourage students to: Name their frog and take it home and show their families and friends how force works.

Force Pop-Up Frog Template

4.4: Slide on Ramp

Time Required	30 min
Group Sizes	1
Grade	PreK - 5
Materials Needed	

- Whiteboard/Markers
- Laptop/Projector
- Ruler / Measuring Tape
- Wooden Ramp
- Toy Cars

Learning Objectives
- Understand that momentum is measured as a product of its mass and velocity.
- Understand that the more an object rolls, the more momentum it will have once it hits another object.
- Understand that an object rolling from a lower incline has less momentum and an object rolling from a higher incline has more momentum.

You can use a wooden slab to make a ramp; or a long book or use a Pipe insulation cut in half long ways. Mark 4 levels on the ramp using masking tape. Level 1 is the lowest, level 4 the highest. On the floor about 3-4 inches in front of the ramp, place a strip of masking tape to mark the spot where a marker will lie or you can use a glue stick.

Ask participants if they roll a toy car or a marble from each level and a marker is lying on the floor, when the marker will move most – when the car is released from level 1, 2, 3, or 4.

After everyone has a hypothesis, have them record their hypothesis. Then test the hypothesis as follows: Participants taking turns roll their car from level 1 (no pushing the car, just let it free roll from the level marker). When the car strikes the marker on the floor, the marker rolls off.

Have participants measure this displacement from the masking tape marking the marker's initial position. Participants record this reading against level 1 on the whiteboard. Repeat for each level. Discuss the results.

Modification for Grades PreK to Second:

For younger participants, you can have them place a piece of masking tape where the marker moves to based on the level the toy car or marble rolls from. Have them write the level number on the tape and discuss the tape placements once all 4 levels have been completed.

You can then have them practice measuring with a ruler - Guide the participants as they try to measure the placement of the tapes. It's okay if the measurements are not perfect as it may be their first time using a ruler.

Repeat the experiment on a different surface (like a table top). So, participants will have 2 data points for each level.

Once the participants have completed the worksheet, either draw or use excel to generate a graph of the average distance that the car made depending on the level.

For example, on level 1, five teams recorded that their cars went 3, 4, 7, 11, and 4 cm before stopping. Together with the class, add all distances together (29) and divide it by the number of teams, or five in this case. Then, the average distance would be 5.8 cm, or rounded 6 cm.

Create a graph with each level shown for a certain surface. Below is an example of an excel graph. Ask questions that you notice about the data.

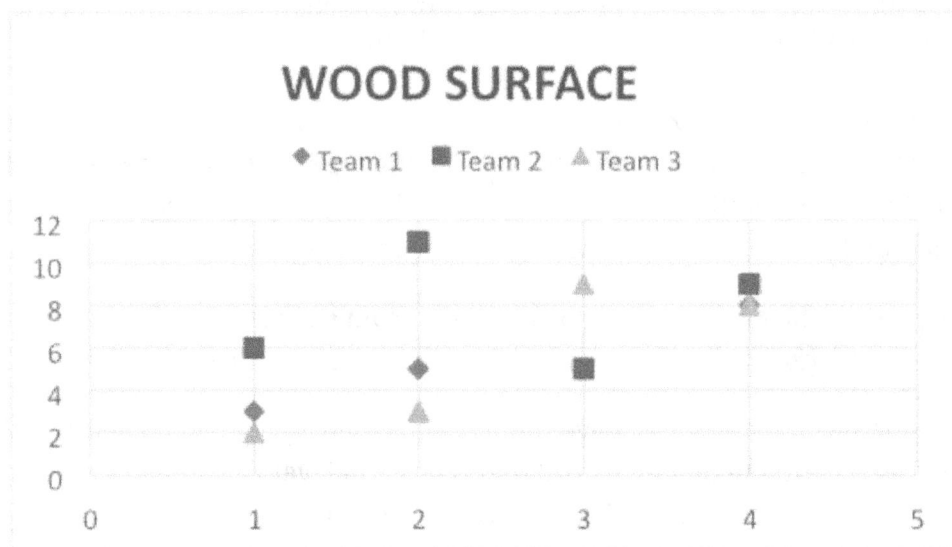

WOOD SURFACE

Explanation

This experiment displays the 2nd law of motion. Car rolling from lower level has less momentum and results in lesser impact (displacement of the marker). Car rolling from the higher level packs in more momentum, leading to a greater impact.

Slide on Ramp

Slide from:	How far did the ground stuff go?	
	Surface 1	Surface 2
First Level		
Second Level		
Third Level		
Fourth Level		

When did the ground stuff move the most?

_____

_____

_____

_____

Why?

_____

_____

_____

_____

4.5: Preparing for the Future: AI Integration & Recap

Time Required	20 min
Group Sizes	1 - 2
Grade	PreK - 5

Learning Objectives
- Explore age-appropriate AI & machine learning to enhance understanding of motion & machines.

Here is a curated list of age-appropriate Artificial Intelligence (AI) / Machine Learning (ML) extensions that naturally build on Module 4 Mechanical Engineering lessons. These are designed to be optional enhancements, scalable from PreK through Grade 5, and aligned with your focus on motion, machines, data, and design thinking.

4.1 Laws of Motion Recap
- Chatbot Recall Coach (PreK–5):
  - Use a teacher-guided chatbot to ask:
    - "What makes something start moving?"
    - "What makes something stop?"
    - "What happens when two objects push each other?"
  - The chatbot reinforces vocabulary (inertia, force, action–reaction) using simple language.

- Law Matching Game with AI (Grades 1–5):
  - Show pictures or short animations (ball rolling, person pushing wall, car stopping).
  - Students label which law applies.
  - Explain that ML learns by matching examples to categories.

- Human vs AI Thinking Discussion (Grades 3–5):
  - Ask:
    - "How do humans remember rules?"
    - "How would a computer remember the laws of motion?"
  - Introduce AI as learning patterns from many examples.

4.2 Law 2 - Explore Forces
- Force Distance Data Chart (Grades 2–5):
  - Record:
    - Object used (paper ball vs ping pong vs rubber ball)
    - Distance traveled
    - Force Applied
  - Create a simple bar chart showing how force and mass affect motion.

- Prediction vs Outcome AI Discussion (Grades 3–5):
  - Compare:
    - Student predictions
    - Measured distances
  - Discuss how AI compares predictions to real data to learn.

- Basketball Distance Tracker (Grades 1–5):
  - Track number of goals as distance increases.
  - Ask:
    - "What changed when the bucket moved farther away?"
  - Connect increasing force to increased distance.

4.3 Force Pop-Up Frog

- Design Thinking Chatbot (PreK–2):
  - Students ask:
    - "What makes my frog jump?"
    - "What happens if I push harder?"
  - The chatbot encourages repeated testing and observation.

- Push Strength Observation Chart (Grades PreK–5):
  - Track:
    - Soft push
    - Medium push
    - Hard push
  - Draw symbols or bars showing jump height.

- Cause-and-Effect AI Talk (Grades 3–5):
  - Ask:
    - "How does the frog know how high to jump?"
  - Explain that AI also reacts to input strength (more input → bigger output).

- Slow-Motion Replay (Teacher-Led):
  - Use a tablet or camera to replay frog jumps.
    - Recommended: Microsoft ClipChamp
  - Discuss how slowing motion helps both scientists and AI notice details.

4.4 Slide on Ramp

- Hypothesis Coach Chatbot (PreK–5):
  - Before testing, students ask:
    - "Which level will push the marker farthest?"
    - "Why do you think that?"
  - The chatbot encourages reasoning before testing.

- Momentum Data Collection (Grades 2–5):
  - Record:
    - Ramp level
    - Distance marker moved
  - Create a class table or spreadsheet.

- Graphing with AI Tools (Grades 3–5):
  - Use Excel or a graph tool to show:
    - Ramp height vs distance moved
  - Discuss how AI reads graphs to find trends.

- Pattern Recognition Discussion (Grades 4–5):
  - Ask:
    - "What happened as the ramp got higher?"
    - "What stayed the same?"
  - Connect to how ML identifies patterns across trials.

Module 5: Farm Truck EDP

This module engages participants in a real-world Engineering Design Process challenge as they design, build, and improve a farm truck that can move and carry a specific load. Through discussion, testing, and iteration, students apply the concept of force to understand how design choices impact movement and performance while working within defined goals, criteria, and constraints.

Materials

Materials for Class:
- Laptop/Projector
- Whiteboard/Markers
- Classroom Supplies like scissors, crayons, markers, tape/masking tape, pencils, construction/printer paper, index cards, etc.
- Recycled materials like boxes, bottles, etc.
- Art Supplies like stickers, washy tape, stamps, pipe cleaners, pom poms, cardstock, popsicle sticks, etc.

Materials for Each Child/Group:
- String
- Straws (2 Each)
- Bottle Caps / Wheels (4 Each)
- Skewers (2 Each)
- Coffee Filters / Cupcake Tins
- Ruler / Measuring Tape (1 Each Group)
- Toy Crops / Vegetables

5.1: Rollin' to the Farm Discussion

Time Required	10 min
Group Sizes	1
Grade	PreK - 5
Materials Needed	

- Whiteboard/Markers
- Laptop/Projector
- Example Farm Truck

Learning Objectives
- Understand the goal is to build a truck that meets specific criteria for movement and load capacity.
- Understand how design choices affect a machine's ability to move and carry objects by testing performance and making improvements based on results and feedback.

Preparation:
Before conducting this activity with students, follow the steps below to build an example truck base to showcase once students start building. Do not add creative details to the truck base so students can still have a blank template to work off of. This project can be done as an engineering design project.

Project Prompt:
Note to Coach: You can change this project prompt to be seasonal by changing the crops the farm is growing at that time of year. For example, autumn can be focused on pumpkins and summer can be focused on tomatoes.

Introduce the project by saying the following:

> "Today, we have been hired by a local farm to help their farmers bring their crops from their farm to their public farm stand! They need help designing and building a truck that can hold either 10 small toy crops or 3 big toy crops.
> This truck will also need to drive to the public farm stand and drop off the crops for all the customers!"

The main parts of their job include:
- Asking the customer (the teacher) the requirements for their designed truck.

- Designing the truck on a piece of paper with the requirements labeled for the customer to review and approve.

- Building the truck based on the requirements.

- Testing the truck to make sure it moves great on a select surface and can hold a certain number of crops.

- Improving the truck based on the results from testing so that the truck can roll well on a select surface and carry the crops.

- Get feedback from the customer on the truck that you designed, built, and tested.

With your students, write on the whiteboard what are the characteristics of a truck and things they should consider while building a machine that can move and hold objects.

Once done, you can begin following the activity to build a truck - Remember, students will need to add to the design for it to work for the crop load. They will be using the Engineering Design Process for this project.

5.2: Farm Truck EDP

Time Required	45 min
Group Sizes	1
Grade	PreK - 5
Materials Needed	

- Whiteboard/Markers
- Laptop/Projector
- String
- Straws (2 Each)
- Bottle Caps / Wheels (4 Each)
- Skewers (2 Each)
- Coffee Filters / Cupcake Tins
- Toy Crops / Vegetables
- Ruler / Measuring Tape (1 Each Group)
- Classroom Supplies like scissors, crayons, markers, tape/masking tape, pencils, construction/printer paper, index cards, etc.
- Recycled materials like boxes, bottles, etc.
- Art Supplies like stickers, washy tape, stamps, pipe cleaners, pom poms, cardstock, popsicle sticks, etc.

Learning Objectives
- Understand how to engineer and design a car that can move by applying the concept of force.
- Understand the application of the engineering design process to certain goals, criteria, and constraints.
- Understand how to use the Engineering & Design Process to work through real world problems.

Goal:
Ask the students what is an acceptable goal for building a farm truck. Make sure they realize that they need to think about what the truck will be able to do once built and add that to goal.

**Make a truck that can move easily on different surfaces and
hold a certain number of crops to deliver to a public farm stand**

Ask / Imagine Stage:
Have the students ask questions about the project. You should answer questions on what materials they can use, the criteria for the project, any constraints they may have with the project, and how they can test the project and know if it works or does not work.

Make a truck out of materials provided:
- Construction Paper

- Index Cards
- String
- Straws
- Bottle Caps / Wheels
- Pipe Cleaners
- Popsicle Sticks
- Skewers
- Coffee Filters / Cupcake Tins
- Recycled materials like boxes, bottles, etc.
- Art Supplies like stickers, washy tape, stamps, pipe cleaners, pom poms, cardstock, popsicle sticks, etc.

Materials to help build but will not be used as part of your design.
- Classroom Supplies like scissors, crayons, markers, tape/masking tape, pencils, construction/printer paper, index cards, etc.

Explain when engineers work their supplies are limited, so they have to plan for a small amount of supplies.

Criteria:
- The truck should not fall apart by itself.
- The truck must be free-standing.
- The truck must have a top where you can place some crops on it.

Constraints:
- Use only the materials as specified.

Test:
- Place the crops on the truck - How many can your truck hold?
- Push the truck from the farm to the public farm stand and see how easily it rolls.
- See if the materials stay together while rolling.

Plan:
For the Plan section, have the students draw out the two designs that they want. These designs will be what we will use for the farm truck. You can use the "My Engineering Design Process" worksheet.

Show participants the available materials. Tell them that they will use the materials to make a truck to take home. They will do this while working as an engineer.

Encourage them to ask questions about the criteria and requirements. Tell them they will only get one set of material per participant.

Ask, what are the main parts of a truck?

- Wheels – so it can roll
- A body where we can attach the wheels
- Bed of the truck to hold the pumpkin load

Point to the "My Engineering Plan" worksheet and have them think about the supplied materials.

Start with the first material on the list, show it to them and ask: What does this material look like? How does it feel? What are its properties? For example for cardstock, feels smooth, it's a rectangular sheet. Feels sturdier than a piece of paper, etc.

After discussion as a group, have participants write their thoughts. Ask, how could you use this material to make a truck? *Used to make the body.* Will you use the full sheet? Have them think it through. *The ideal solution is to cut the sheet to make a smaller rectangular body.*

Ask, what would they need to cut? *Scissors.* Tell them they can get scissors if they need. How else could the material be used to make the truck? *Make wheels.* Do they have something else to make wheels? *A template to trace/cut circles and scissors.*

Note to Coach: You can coach them through any materials to use for the wheels like bottle caps or wooden circles.

Now, we want to plan out the bed of the truck for the crop load. The truck will need to pull multiple loads of crops from the farm to the public farm stand. Have the students think about the materials needed to hold the crop load.

Continue, in an inquiry based manner so participants can figure out ways to use the materials supplied. After a common discussion, have the groups reflect and complete the materials analysis. Afterwards, have the teams draw out a diagram /plan of how their trucks might look. Make sure the students note down the materials they are using, how much material they are using, and where on the truck each material will be.

Once students have completed their plan, they must seek approval from the teacher before beginning to build. Review the plan, ask clarifying questions. Ensure that they have considered all facts and have a reasonable plan to make a truck. Once satisfied with the plan, ask them what materials they need and supply them with the materials. You can use a sticker or a simple check mark to write on their plan as approval.

My Engineering Design Process

Did it work?
YES: How can it be better?
NO: How can we fix it?

What do we have to work with and
what do we want it to do?

Improve

Ask

The Goal:

What have we
learned to
complete this
challenge?

Create

Imagine

Build it!

Plan

Draw out a few ideas on how to
complete this challenge:

My Engineering Design Plan

Material	Properties	How could you use it in your design?

Draw a possible solution:

Car Wheels Template

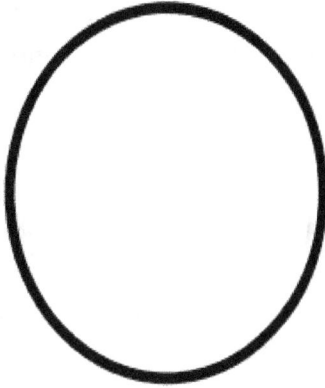

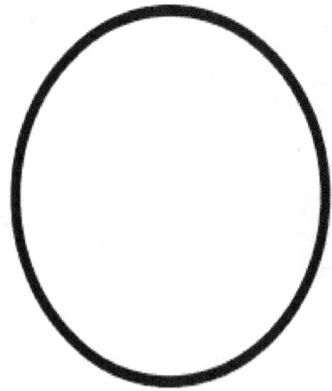

Build

Note to Coach: For younger groups, each participant can make one type of design, and in a group, they can test out different trucks as time allows.

Participants working in teams need to make one truck for each participant in the team. Encourage them to make one truck, make sure it works fine and then replicate that design for others in the team. Or, improvise as needed for the next truck. After they have tested their first design, allow the students to improve their design or try a different design.

See the picture below on how to make the base of the truck. You can see that the axle connected to the wheels should be able to move freely. The index card here is rolled over the axle but NOT taped to the axle. (Please see the video for exact steps on making the base of the truck in the STEM For Kids Digital Library.)

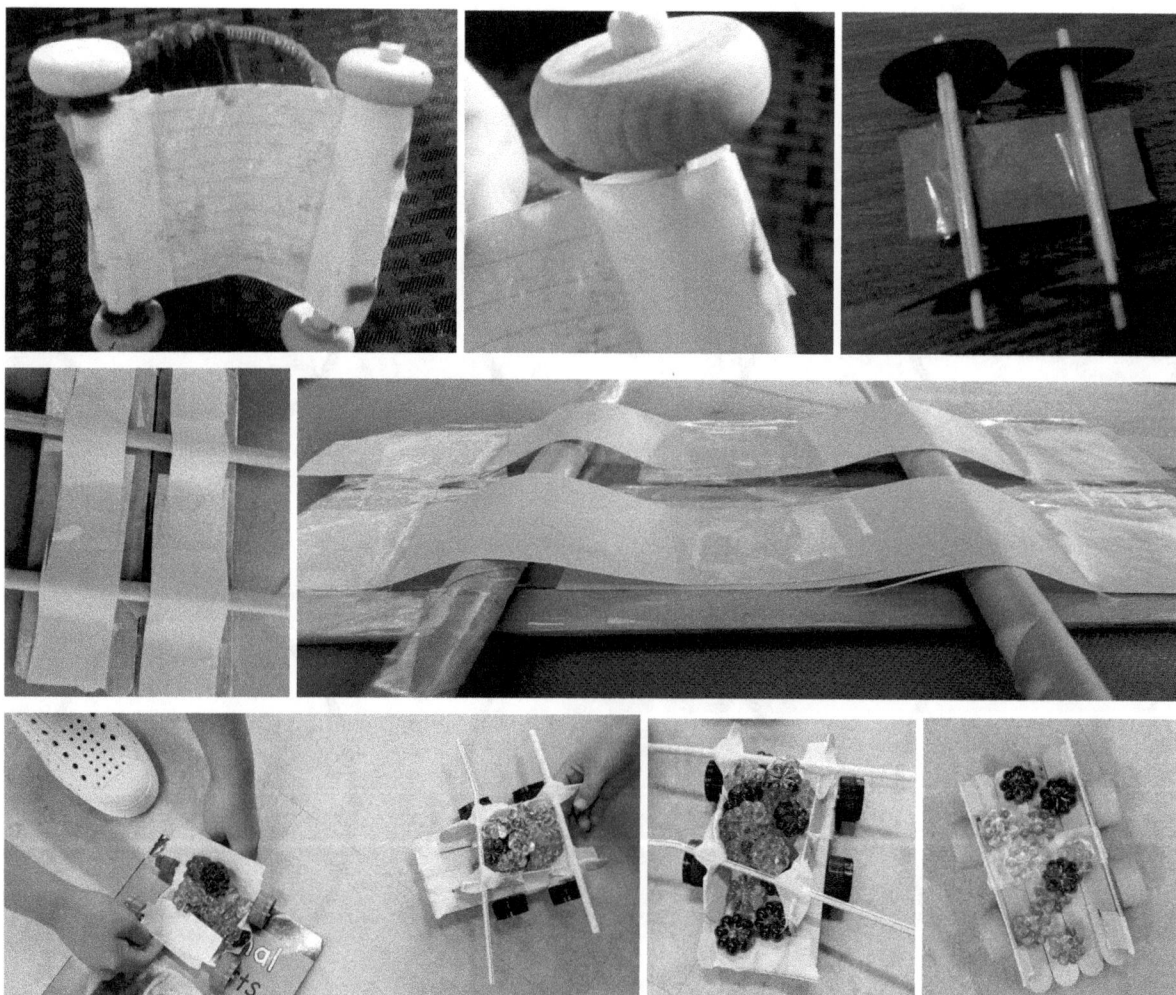

Test

When they have built the truck, test the truck by pushing to see that it is able to roll easily. Improve the friction on the wheels to get the truck moving further on a select surface.

- Place the toy crops on the truck - How many can your truck hold?
- Push the truck from the farm to the public farm stand and see how easily it rolls.
- See if the materials stay together while rolling.
- Add the toy / decor crops to the bed of the truck one at a time. Pull the truck with the same force each time until you cannot pull the truck anymore. What is happening to the forces between the truck and crops? Between the truck and the surface it is on? At that point, the friction from the surface that the truck is on is greater than the force from your truck/hand pulling the truck.

Extension

Have the participants' think of different ways to get their trucks moving. Have a box of materials on the side for them to use to make a new way.

Note to Coach: Let participants' creativity take shape. In case students need help you can offer ideas. Below are a few ideas for creation.

Note to Coach: You can have the students measure the distance their truck can travel depending on how many crops are in the truck bed to see how the force affects the wheels of the truck.

STEM Farm

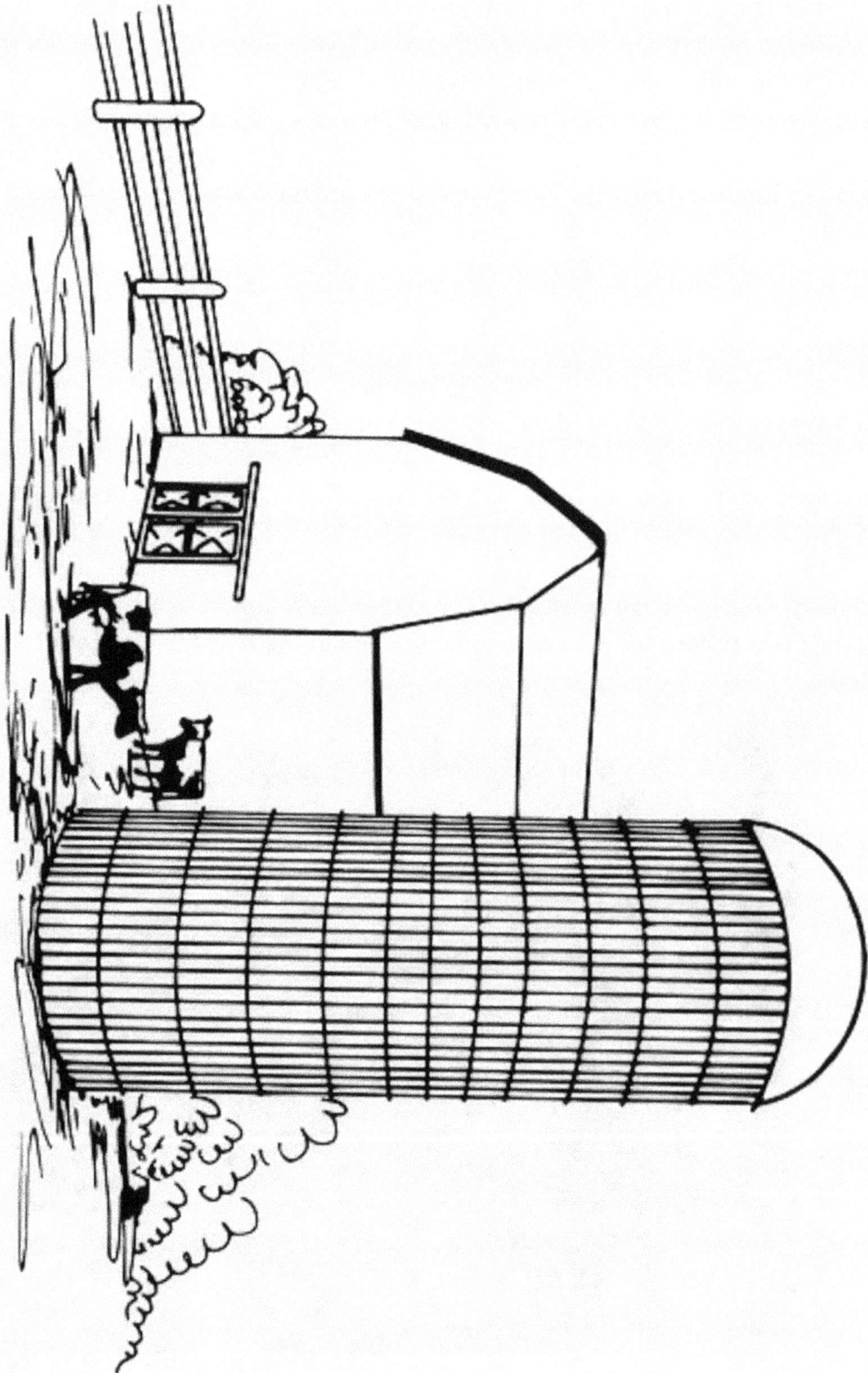

Public Farm Stand

80¢

PUMPKINS 4 SALE

Improve

Students will be able to improve their truck designs. They can also see if changing the material used will improve their truck's movement. Allow them to change their second design if they feel like it would not work like they originally thought based on the results from the first design.

Communications

Have each student come up to the front and showcase their design. They should talk about how many crops their truck moved to the public farm stand. You can also ask them what was the easiest/hardest part of their design and how they might improve their design in the future. You can provide a prize or sticker as compensation for completing the project.

Extensions

Run a contest for the best truck. Place 3 categories on the board: AESTHETIC, LOAD ABILITY, FUNCTION. Students who want to participate can have the teacher rate their trucks from 1 to 5, 1 being low and 5 being high. Explain why you are giving a certain score as you write it on the board.

Note to Coach: Make sure to try to find something positive to say about each truck. You can even open the floor for other students to say a positive thing about a truck as it is being shown.

5.3: Preparing for the Future: AI Integration & Recap

Time Required	20 min
Group Sizes	1 - 2
Grade	PreK - 5

<u>Learning Objectives</u>
- Explore age-appropriate AI & machine learning to enhance understanding of motion & machines.

Here is a curated list of age-appropriate Artificial Intelligence (AI) / Machine Learning (ML) extensions that naturally build on Module 5 Mechanical Engineering lessons.

These are designed to be optional enhancements, scalable from PreK through Grade 5, and aligned with your focus on motion, machines, data, and design thinking.

5.1 Rollin' to the Farm Discussion

- Engineering Chatbot: "The Customer" (PreK–5):
    - Use a teacher-guided chatbot to role-play the farmer asking:
        - "How many crops does your truck need to carry?"
        - "How will your truck move from the farm to the stand?"
        - "What happens if it carries too much?"
    - Students learn how engineers gather requirements from a customer.

- Design Choice Predictor (Grades 2–5):
    - Ask a chatbot:
        - "What might happen if my truck has small wheels?"
        - "What if my truck bed is too tall?"
    - Discuss that AI makes predictions based on patterns it has learned from past designs.

- Example vs Non-Example Analysis (Grades K–5):
    - Show images of:
        - Trucks that roll well
        - Trucks that don't roll well
    - Explain that ML learns by comparing examples, just like engineers compare designs.

5.2 Farm Truck EDP

Ask / Imagine Stage

- Question Generator Chatbot (PreK–5):
    - Students ask:
        - "What materials are strong?"
        - "What helps wheels spin?"
        - "How can I keep my truck from tipping?"
    - The chatbot models curiosity, not answers.

- Material Property Analyzer (Grades 2–5):
    - Input material observations (strong, bendy, smooth) into a shared chart.
    - Discuss how ML learns from labeled data like this.

Plan Stage

- AI Planning Partner (Grades 3–5):
    - Students ask:
        - "Where should the wheels go?"
        - "How big should the truck bed be?"
    - AI helps students think through tradeoffs before building.

- Digital Sketch + Annotation (Teacher-led):
    - Use a tablet or projector to annotate a sample truck plan.
        - Recommended: Google Gemini
    - Explain how AI uses diagrams and labeled parts to understand designs.

Build Stage

- Build Reflection Chatbot (PreK–5):
  - Mid-build prompts:
    - "What part was hardest to make?"
    - "What is working well so far?"
  - Helps students pause and reflect like engineers.

- Replication & Pattern Talk (Grades 3–5):
  - Compare multiple trucks built with similar plans.
  - Discuss how ML notices similarities across designs.

Test Stage

- Data Collection Table (Grades 1–5):
  - Track:
    - Number of crops carried
    - Distance rolled
    - Surface type
  - Explain that AI improves by learning from test results.

- Graphing with AI Tools (Grades 2–5):
  - Create:
    - Bar graph: Crops vs Distance
    - Chart: Wheel type vs Performance
  - Discuss how AI uses graphs to find patterns.

- Prediction vs Outcome Discussion (Grades 3–5):
  - Compare:
    - What students expected vs What actually happened
  - Explain that AI adjusts predictions based on new data.

Improve Stage

- Design Improvement Chatbot (PreK–5):
  - Students ask:
    - "How can I reduce friction?"
    - "What could make my truck stronger?"
  - Reinforces iterative design.

- Before & After Comparison (Grades 2–5):
  - Create a simple comparison chart:
    - Original design
    - Improved design
  - Explain how ML improves by learning from earlier versions.

Communicate Stage

- AI Interviewer (Grades 3–5):
  - Chatbot asks students:
    - "What problem did your truck solve?"
    - "What would you change next time?"
  - Models professional engineering reflection.

Module 6: Action - Reaction Motion

This module explores Newton's Third Law of Motion by helping participants understand action and reaction through engaging, hands-on experiments and design challenges. Through activities such as balloon rockets, cup poppers, and engineering a block car, students observe how equal and opposite forces create motion, and how changes in force and materials affect results. The module reinforces all three laws of motion while applying the Engineering Design Process to real-world mechanical systems.

Materials

Materials for Class:

- Laptop/Projector
- Whiteboard/Markers
- Classroom Supplies like scissors, crayons, markers, tape/masking tape, pencils, construction/printer paper, index cards, etc.
- Recycled materials like boxes, bottles, etc.
- Art Supplies like stickers, washy tape, stamps, pipe cleaners, pom poms, cardstock, popsicle sticks, etc.
- Lego-Type Block Pieces

Materials for Each Child/Group:

- String
- Straws (1 Each)
- Balloons (2 Each)
- Ruler / Measuring Tape (1 Each Group)
- Lego-Type Block Wheels
- Lego-Type Block Axles
- Disc Shooters (1 Each)
- Bouncy Balls (1 Each)
- Small Cups (1 Each)
- Pom Poms (1 Each)

6.1: Laws of Motion Recap

Time Required	15 min
Group Sizes	1
Grade	PreK - 5
Materials Needed	
• Whiteboard/Markers • Laptop/Projector	

Learning Objectives
- Understand that there are three laws of motion: Inertia, Force, and Action-Reaction.

Newton's Three Laws of Motion
1. Everything is lazy, doesn't move unless a force is applied – Inertia
2. More force is needed to move heavier objects or to go farther
3. For every action, there is an equal and opposite reaction

Play a recap game to ensure participants remember the essence of the three laws.

Summarize the Three Laws of Motion

Who made the 3 laws of motion?

_____

What are the three laws?

Law	What is it?	What did I play with to learn about this law?
1.		
2.		
3.		

6.2: Law 3 - Balloon Rocket

Time Required	15 min
Group Sizes	1
Grade	PreK - 5
Materials Needed	
• Whiteboard/Markers • Laptop/Projector • Balloons	

Learning Objectives
- Understand that an action is a force that pushes or pulls on an object.
- Understand that a reaction is the equal push or pull of an object in the opposite direction.
- Understand that the action of letting go of a balloon is when the air rushes out and the reaction is the balloon moving forward.
- Understand that action-reaction does not occur when a tied balloon is let go because no air can escape.

Take a balloon, fill air and hold tightly at the nozzle. Show the balloon to the participants and ask what will happen if you let go of the balloon. *Take responses.* They may say it will fall down, slowly fall down like a feather.

Let go of the balloon. *The balloon flies like a rocket, traverses a path as air empties and then once all air is out, falls to the ground.*

Action is defined as a force that pushes or pulls on an object.

Ask participants what is the action of the balloon? *When we let it go, air rushes out.* Explain that rushing out of air is the action.

Reaction is defined as the equal push or pull of an object in the opposite direction.

Ask participants what was the reaction here? *The balloon blasts forward.*

Take a balloon, blow it up and tie its end. Now ask participants what will happen if we let it go. Let go of the balloon. Explain this balloon will just fall (slowly floating) to the ground. Ask participants to explain the difference between the two.

Hand the participants their own balloon and ask them to blow it up. Explain that we do not want to let it go until it is time to. On the count of three, we will all say action reaction really fast just like the balloon does when the air goes out and the balloon flies.

Third Law of Motion Comprehension
Explain, this is the final law of motion: "Every action has an equal and opposite reaction." For our balloon, the action is the air rushing out and the reaction is the way the balloon moves forward. Also note that the reaction is only equal to the amount of air we blow into the balloon.

6.3: Disc Shooter & Bouncy Balls

Time Required	15 min
Group Sizes	1
Grade	PreK - 5
Materials Needed	

- Whiteboard/Markers
- Laptop/Projector
- Disc Shooters
- Bouncy Balls

Learning Objectives
- Understand that the action of a disc shooter is the force applied when pinching right at the disc and the reaction is the disc flying out of the handle.
- Understand that the action of bouncing a ball is the force of gravity when the ball hits the ground and the reaction is the ball bouncing back from the ground.
- Understand how speed, timing, and angle can change the reaction of their action.

Bouncy Ball Action-Reaction

Take two rubber balls or marbles and roll one into the other one (while it is still). Ask participants, what happens? *The one that's hit moves. The one we rolled stops and moves in the opposite direction.*

Ask participants to explain this using Newton's third law of motion. *The action of the rolling ball causes the still ball to move in the direction of the force (This is the second law) and the original rolling ball moves in the opposite direction (third law).*

Take a bouncing ball and hit it on the floor. The harder you hit the more it bounces back. Action is you throwing the ball to the floor and reaction is the ball bouncing back.

Bouncy-Catch Game

Pair up participants. Give each pair a bouncing ball. Each pair stands 5 – 8 feet away facing each other. A participant passes the ball to his/her teammate and the teammate catches the ball. The important condition is the ball must hit the ground once and should be thrown at an angle such that after bouncing back it continues towards the other participant.

If available, provide each participant a bouncing ball to try it out. Or, take participants to a ball court and dribble with a basketball or a similar ball.

Bouncy Target Game

Draw a target on displayed newspaper with different point values. The newspaper should be attached at about waist level on walls. For bigger groups, draw multiple targets.

The targets can be concentric circles – the outer one with a low value like 10 points; gradually increase points; the smallest inside circle should have maximum points 1000.

Group participants into 6-8 and have them stand in front of the target about 5 feet away. They can then "shoot" their bouncy balls to see how many times they can score 1000. Remember that the balls must bounce off the floor to hit the target. No direct throws are allowed. Make it a timed play, if needed or just free play time.

Participants would need to fine tune their angle of throw, speed and distance to hit the targets. After the game, ask them about what characteristics of their throw they try to tweak to make the target.

Disc Shooter Exploration

If available, provide participants a disc shooter to experience action and reaction. Have it where, as the participants pinch the disc shooter, they yell "Action!" and as the participants see the disc fly, they yell "Reaction!"

CAUTION: Ensure that discs are shot away from people.

6.4: Action Reaction Cup Poppers

Time Required	30 min
Group Sizes	1
Grade	PreK - 5
Materials Needed	

- Whiteboard/Markers
- Laptop/Projector
- Small Cups
- Balloons
- Pom Poms
- Scissors
- Tape
- Ruler / Measuring Tape

Learning Objectives

- Understand that the action of a popper with a pom-pom inside is the pulling and releasing of the balloon and the reaction is the pom-pom shooting some distance.
- Understand that the distance the pom-pom flies is equal to the force we pulled back on the balloon.
- Understand that the pom-pom will go a far distance if the balloon is pulled back far and the pom-pom will go a short distance if the balloon is pulled back short.

Prompt:

At the beginning of this lesson, have the participants sit in front of you and tell them what they are going to do today:

> It was the snowiest day of the year in Motionville, and all the kids were outside building snowmen, making snow angels, and having epic snowball fights. Suddenly, BOOM! A loud crash echoed across the town.
>
> Out of the sky, spinning like a top, came a bright, flashing figure wearing shiny silver pants and a cape that flapped in the wind. It was none other than... Captain EnergyPants!
>
> "Kids of Energyville! We have a big problem!" he shouted, landing in a superhero pose. "The Slush Monster from Iceberg Island is stomping toward town, and if he reaches us, he'll turn all our snow into yucky, slushy goo!"
>
> The kids gasped. "But what can we do, Captain?"
>
> "You must build a SNOWBALL LAUNCHER!" Captain EnergyPants said. "It's the only way to stop him before he gets too close!"

Show the participants a model of the cup popper they will be building next. Have the pom-pom fly into the classroom to generate excitement. Explain that you pull back the knot part of the balloon and let go to allow it to hit the pom-pom, making it fly through the air.

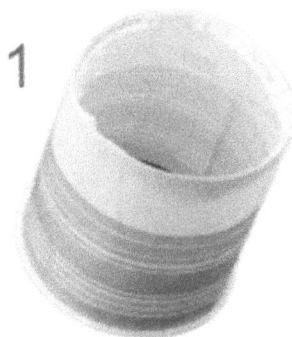

Step 1: Take a small cup and cut out the part at the bottom which helps hold the liquid in a cup. Make sure the cutting is somewhat even.

Step 2: On a balloon, tie a knot at the mouth piece. Make sure the participants do not blow up their balloons at all to keep the inside dry. Cut about half an inch from the top of the balloon so that one end is open and the other is knotted off.

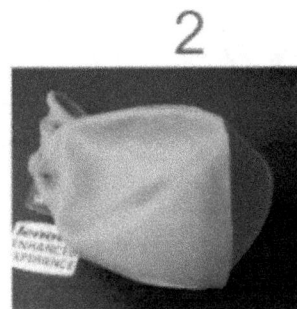

Step 3: Stretch the open end over the open bottom of the cup. The cup should be now closed off with the knot in the middle.

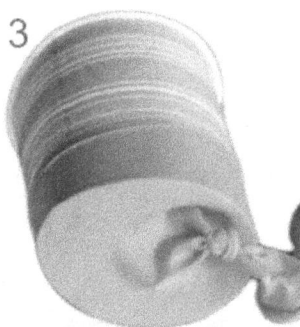

NOTE TO COACH: You may have to secure the balloon to the cup if the knot is too close to the cut made on the balloon. Make sure the participants keep the knot closer to the end of the mouth piece.

Step 4: Place the pom-pom inside of the cup, touching the balloon end. Pull back the knot and let it go. The pom-pom should fly out of the cup!

Draw a target on the whiteboard and play a game of target practice. Have the circle in the middle be worth 5 points and each bigger circle after worth 4, 3, 2, and 1 points.

Play a game of tag with the cup popper. Make sure you are in an open area and watch the participants carefully. As they pull the knot, they should say "Action" and when the pom-pom flies, they should say "Reaction!"

The Slush Monster

Experiment

Have the participants measure how far their cup popper can get their pom-pom to go with different forces. We will be trying 3 different forces or pulls of the balloon knot to see the distance. Have the participants get into groups of two.

Prompt the participants to stand on a piece of paper which will be their starting point. Have the pom-pom in the cup. Participants will pull the balloon knot just an inch to try the smallest force to get the pom-pom to move. Their partner will count down to when they should let go of the knot. Together, they will measure how far the pom-pom flew from the start point to the pom-pom.

On the worksheet, the participants can write their results. They will need to do each force 3 times. Once the first force has been done 3 times, have the participants add up the three numbers and divide that sum by 3 to find the mean of the distance. Have the participants find the median of the results by putting the numbers in order and circling the number in the middle. Prompt the participants to find the mode. If there are no repeating numbers, there is no mode.

Extension for Grades 2 to 5:

Draw out the following chart on the board and have the participants fill out the chart as they do the experiment.

Team Name	1 Inch Pull	2 Inch Pull	3 Inch Pull
Blue Team	Mean: Median: Mode:	Mean: Median: Mode:	Mean: Median: Mode:
Red Team	Mean: Median: Mode:	Mean: Median: Mode:	Mean: Median: Mode:

Have the participants write their results on the whiteboard. They will do two more forces of 2 inch pull and 3 inch pull.

Draw out or use excel to create a graph of every teams' median for each pull. Use a different shape or color for each pull. See if there are any similarities or differences that can be seen based on the forces done.

Popper Power

Discover which pull on the balloon knot is best for the cup popper to get the pom-pom to fly the most distance.

Pull on the Balloon Knot	Distance flew Test #1	Distance flew Test #2	Distance flew Test #3	Results
1 inch				Mean: Median: Mode:
2 inch				Mean: Median: Mode:
3 inch				Mean: Median: Mode:

Which pull makes the pom-pom go the farthest? _____

Why do you think this pull made the pom-pom go the farthest?

_____

_____

_____

_____

6.5: Action Reaction Block Car

Time Required	30 - 45 min
Group Sizes	1 - 3
Grade	PreK - 5
Materials Needed	

- Whiteboard/Markers
- Laptop/Projector
- Lego-Type Blocks (Including Wheels)
- Straws
- Balloons
- Scissors
- Tape

Learning Objectives

- Understand how to engineer and design a car that can move by applying the concept of action-reaction.
- Understand the importance of material property when building a moving object.
- Understand the application of the engineering design process to certain goals, criteria, and constraints.

Recap what is the third law of motion – Action Reaction!

The goal of this activity is to get the speedy cars to move without pushing or blowing on the car.

Goal: Make a car out of materials provided:

- Lego-Type Block Pieces
- Lego-Type Block Wheels
- Lego-Type Block Axles
- Balloon
- Straw
- Tape

Explain when engineers work their supplies are limited, so they have to plan for a small amount of supplies.

Criteria:

- The car should not fall apart by itself.
- It must be free-standing.
- It must have a top that allows a surface to place some light materials on it.

Constraints

- Use only the materials as specified.

Using what the participants know about action reaction, remind them that the name of this activity is "action-reaction" car.

What does action-reaction remind them of? *One of Newton's laws.*

What activities did we do to learn about this law? *Bouncy ball game. Balloon rocket.*

What ideas do they have to use action-reaction and balloon to power their car? *Remind them that air flowing out of the balloon will push the car in the opposite direction.*

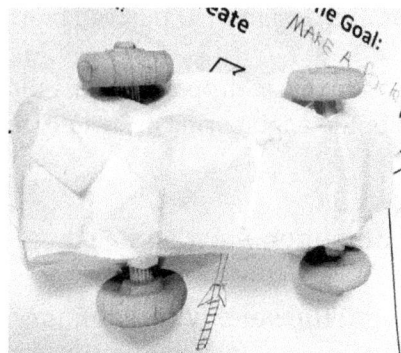

My Engineering Design Process

Did it work?
YES: How can it be better?
NO: How can we fix it?

What do we have to work with and
what do we want it to do?

Improve

Ask

The Goal:

What have we
learned to
complete this
challenge?

Create

Imagine

Build it!

Plan

Draw out a few ideas on how to
complete this challenge:

My Engineering Design Plan

Material	Properties	How could you use it in your design?

Draw a possible solution:

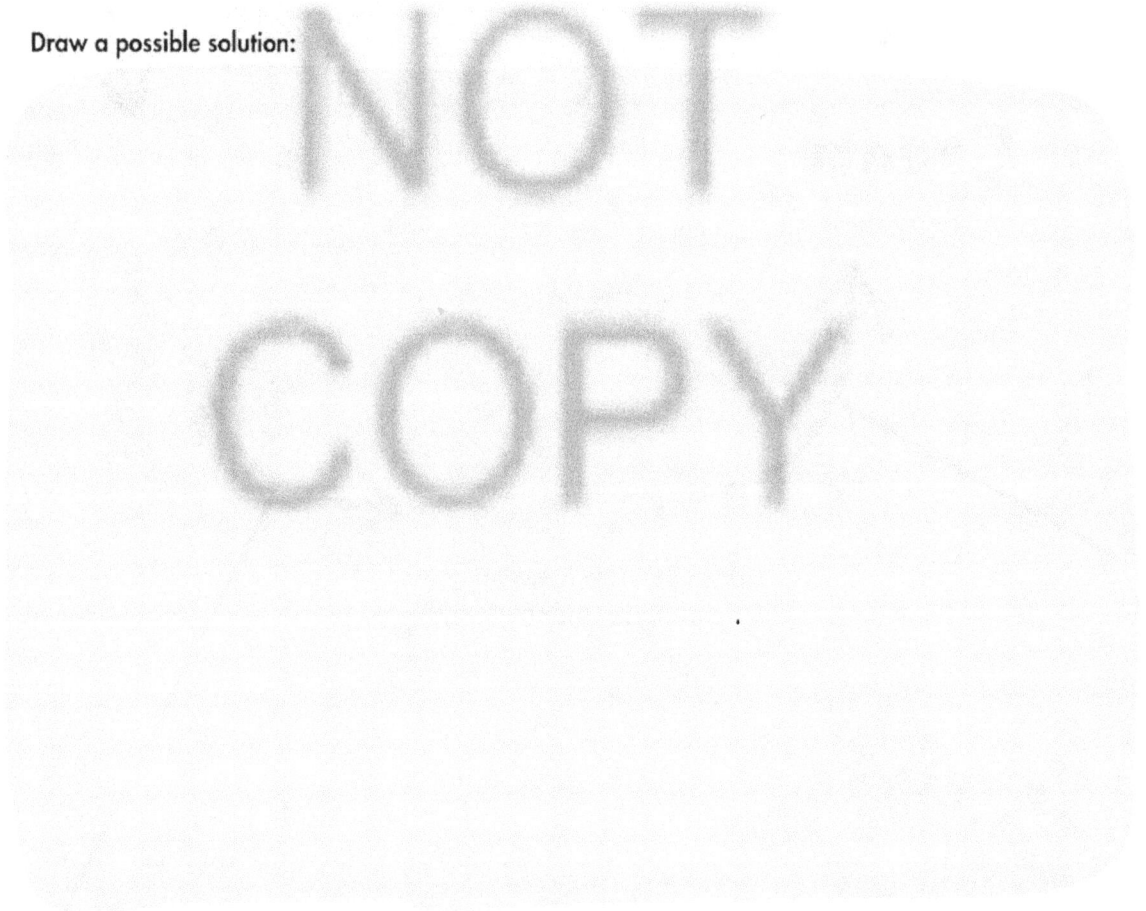

Once, they can visualize the approach of making their powered cars, have them think about how they could attach the balloon to their speedy cars.

Have them think about how they could inflate the balloon frequently without having to attach and detach the balloon from the car.

Once the participants have a reasonable plan, give them the materials to make the balloon attachment to power the car. They can use a straw, balloon, tape, and string.

As cars are completed, have participants measure how far the car goes. Have them think about ways to improve and increase the traveled distance.

After all the cars are complete, have a car race. Mark a starting line using masking tape. Have all participants line up on the starting line.

Get them to position up their cars (i.e. inflate the balloons) and get ready for the race.

6.6: Pom Pom Target Practice

Time Required	15 min
Group Sizes	1
Grade	PreK - 5
Materials Needed	

- Whiteboard/Markers
- Laptop/Projector
- Popsicle Stick
- Pom Pom

Learning Objectives
- Understand that there is a distinction between force (applying) and action-reaction (resulting from application) when getting an object moving.

Take a craft stick and a pom-pom; make a pom-pom catapult off the stick by pressing the stick down on one end while firmly holding the other end of the stick with the other hand.

The action on the stick creates the reaction of the pompom flying off.

Make a distinction between action-reaction (3rd law) and direct force (2nd law). With Straw rockets, blowing into the straws created a direct force that moved the straw rocket. Whereas, with the pom-pom catapult, the force is applied in pushing the catapult down that generates a reactionary force that sends the pom-pom flying off.

Hand each participant a pom-pom and a craft stick. Have them carefully and firmly hold the craft stick at one end with one hand. Place pom-pom on the other hand and push the stick

93

down using the other hand (at the pom-pom end) and release, still holding on to the other hand with the other hand.

The pom-pom bounces off and flies through the air.

Draw a target on a white board (or displayed piece of paper) with different point values. For bigger groups and bigger whiteboards, draw multiple targets.

The targets can be concentric circles – the outer one with a low value like 10 points; gradually increase points; the smallest inside circle should have maximum points 1000.

Group participants into 6-8 and have them stand in front of the target about 5 feet away. They can then "shoot" their pom-poms to see how many times they can score 1000. Make it a timed play, if needed or just free play time.

Target the Coach
Ask each group of participants to stand in a line (one row) facing their program coach about 5-6 feet away. They can then try to tag their coach using their action-reaction pom-pom catapult. Reiterate that they need to be extra cautious not to let go off their craft sticks. Let participants have fun and enjoy the action-reaction experience.

Catapult Tag
Use the catapult to play a game of tag. Tagged participants have to sit down on the floor until the person who tagged them gets tagged by someone else. That's when they get up and continue playing.

6.7: Bowling With Newton

Time Required	15 min
Group Sizes	1
Grade	PreK - 5
Materials Needed	
• Whiteboard/Markers • Laptop/Projector	

Learning Objectives
- Understand that there are three laws of motion: Inertia, Force, and Action-Reaction.
- Understand how the three laws of motion are working in a situation through reading comprehension.

Have participants read the Bowling with Newton passage and record answers. Discuss as a group once everyone is done.

Bowling With Newton

WOOSH! The bowler pushes the ball down the alley, it curves to the left, hits the rack of pins, pushes the pins to the side, and all the pins go down...STRIKE!

A lot of people love to bowl, but have you ever wondered about the science behind it? After all, the moving ball only hits a few pins, but they all can fall down at once.

This motion can be described using a very famous set of rules called *Newton's laws of motion*.

We all know the story of the apple falling on Sir Isaac Newton's head, but he also created three laws to help explain this and all other types of motion.

If we were to go bowling, would the ball on the rack move without anyone touching it? Why not?

This is because an object can only move if a *force* is put on it. For example, our bowling ball moves because you push it down the alley. This is the first law in Newton's three laws of motion.

Our bowling ball, when pushed down the alley, is speeding up toward the pins. This forward motion is in the same direction of the force of the ball, because the direction of the speed of an object in motion is the direction of the force being put on that object. This is Newton's second law of motion.

When the ball finally speeds up and hits the bowling pins, what happens?

BAM! The pins are hit by the force of the ball. This same force is transferred through the pins and results in the pins pushing on other pins, making them fall down. This describes Newton's third law, for every action there is a reaction.

As you learn more about mechanical motion, think about how a force is affecting the objects around it and what the reaction to the force might be.

*Directions: From the passage above, use the space below to summarize in your own words **Newton's three laws of motions**.*

1) _____

_____

2) _____

_____

3) _____

_____

6.8: Preparing for the Future: AI Integration & Recap

Time Required	20 min
Group Sizes	1 - 2
Grade	PreK - 5

Learning Objectives
- Explore age-appropriate AI & machine learning to enhance understanding of motion & machines.

Here is a curated list of age-appropriate Artificial Intelligence (AI) / Machine Learning (ML) extensions that naturally build on Module 6 Mechanical Engineering lessons. These are designed to be optional enhancements, scalable from PreK through Grade 5, and aligned with your focus on motion, machines, data, and design thinking.

6.1 Laws of Motion Recap
- Law Matching Game with AI Sorting (Grades K–5):
  - Students match scenarios (ball rolling, balloon flying, object stopping) to:
    - Inertia
    - Force
    - Action–Reaction
  - Explain that ML also learns by matching examples to categories.

- Animated Motion Scenarios:
  - Create short animations of objects starting, stopping, or colliding and showcasing the laws of motion. (Scratch Jr / Scratch)
  - Pause and ask:
    - "Which law do you see here?"
  - Explain how computers analyze motion frame by frame.

- Human vs AI Thinking Discussion (Grades 3–5):
  - Compare:
    - How students explain motion using words
  - How AI identifies motion using patterns and rules

6.2 Law 3 - Balloon Rocket
- Tied vs Untied Balloon Comparison Tool (Grades 2–5):
  - Create a simple chart:
    - Balloon tied → no motion
    - Balloon untied → motion
  - Explain that AI learns by comparing "works" vs "does not work."

- Action–Reaction Animation Builder:
  - Use block-based animation (Scratch Jr / Scratch) to show:
    - Air going backward
    - Balloon moving forward
  - Connect animation steps to cause-and-effect logic.

- Force Amount Discussion (Grades 3–5):
  - Ask:
    - "What happens if we add more air?"
  - Explain that AI predictions improve when more data (air amount) is added.
- Action-Reaction Application (Grades preK–5):
  - Brainstorm in groups about where do we see A/R in real-life
  - Compare results by asking a chatbot for answers.
  - Have each child share an "Aha" learning about A/R use.

6.3 Disc Shooter & Bouncy Balls

- Throw Angle Analyzer (Grades 2–5):
  - Track:
    - Throw angle
    - Bounce distance
    - Target hits
  - Create a simple chart and discuss how AI looks for patterns in movement.

- Slow-Motion Replay (Teacher-led):
  - Use video playback to slow down:
    - Ball hitting the floor
    - Disc leaving the shooter
  - Recommended: https://teachablemachine.withgoogle.com/
  - Explain how AI analyzes motion by breaking it into tiny moments.

- Pattern Recognition Talk (Grades 4–5):
  - Ask:
    - "Which throws worked best?"
    - "What angles scored the most?"
  - Explain how ML finds trends in data like this.

6.4 Action Reaction Cup Poppers

- Distance Data Collection + AI Charts (Grades 2–5):
  - Input pull distance and pom-pom distance into:
    - Bar graphs
    - Line graphs
  - Explain how AI uses graphs to make predictions.

- Mean / Median / Mode Visualizer (Grades 3–5):
  - Use a spreadsheet or chart tool to visualize averages.
  - Discuss how AI summarizes many results into useful information.

- Target Accuracy Analysis (Grades 4–5):
  - Compare:
    - Force used
    - Accuracy on target
  - Explain how ML balances power and precision.

6.5 Action Reaction Block Car

- Material Property Labeling (Grades 2–5):
  - Create a shared chart:
    - Strong
    - Flexible
    - Smooth
  - Explain how ML learns from labeled data.

- Distance Prediction Tool (Grades 3–5):
  - Before racing, students predict distances.
  - After racing, compare predictions to results and revise thinking.

- Design Version Comparison (Grades 4–5):
  - Track:
    - Version 1 vs Version 2
    - Distance traveled
  - Explain how AI improves by learning from earlier versions.

6.6 Pom Pom Target Practice

- Accuracy Tracking Chart (Grades 2–5):
  - Record:
    - Number of hits
    - Score totals
  - Discuss how AI evaluates performance over time.

- Angle Experimentation Tool (Grades 3–5):
  - Change stick angle and record results.
  - Explain how ML tests many variables to find what works best.

- Game Strategy Reflection (Grades 4–5):
  - Ask:
    - "What strategy improved your score?"
  - Connect strategy optimization to AI learning loops.

Module 7: The Dart Challenge

This module explores Newton's three laws of motion—Inertia, Force, and Action-Reaction—by making and flying paper and magazine darts. They measure distances, analyze results with charts, and see how force affects motion, reinforcing both hands-on learning and basic data analysis skills.

Materials

Materials for Class:
- Laptop/Projector
- Whiteboard/Markers
- Classroom Supplies like scissors, crayons, markers, tape/masking tape, pencils, construction/printer paper, index cards, etc.

Materials for Each Child/Group:
- Magazines
- Newspapers
- Ruler / Measuring Tape (1 Each Group)

7.1: The Dart Challenge

Time Required	1 hr 30 min
Group Sizes	2 - 3
Grade	PreK - 5
Materials Needed	

- Whiteboard/Markers
- Laptop/Projector
- Printer Paper
- Ruler
- Magazines
- Newspaper

Learning Objectives
- Understand that there are three laws of motion: Inertia, Force, and Action-Reaction.
- Understand how the three laws of motion are working in a situation through reading comprehension.

Ask participants what they recall about motion from previous modules. *Probe them for Newton's three laws. Take participants' responses and note them on the whiteboard or central display:*

- Everything is lazy, doesn't move unless a force is applied – Inertia
- More force is needed to move heavier objects or to go farther
- For every action, there is an equal and opposite reaction

Give each participant a sheet of printer paper. <u>Watch the "Make a paper dart" Video on the STEM For Kids Digital Library.</u> Explain to participants the intent of several folds in this dart design is to eliminate aerodynamics as much as possible so we can focus on force and effect of force in traveled distance. (We want our dart to go as far as possible.)

Note to Coach: Be sure to watch the video prior to working with participants on dart. You may need to help fold darts for younger participants.

After all the darts are complete, move to a long corridor / hallway. Mark the starting line using masking tape. Have one participant come to the starting line at a time and release their dart. Prompt one participant to start the stopwatch when the flier releases their dart and stop the stopwatch when the dart hits the ground. Record the time on their sheet.

Have the flier measure the distance while the next person in line holds the end of the tape measure and record their distance on their sheet. Make sure that they round their times and distances up or down to a whole number.

Repeat for each participant, 2-4 times. Each participant should get 3-5 turns flying. Encourage them to beat their last distance. Ask how could they do that? *More force.*

Note to Coach: If you have multiple tape measures and stop watches, participants can do the activity in groups. Once printer paper darts have gone five rounds, have participants make magazine paper darts and complete the same process.

The Dart Challenge Worksheet

Round	1	2	3	4	5
Paper Dart Time (seconds)					
Paper Dart Distance (inches)					
Magazine Paper Dart Time (seconds)					
Magazine Paper Dart Distance (inches)					

What was your longest distance? _____

What was your shortest distance? _____

What was your median (middle) distance? _____

Which type of paper dart flew the furthest? (Circle One)

Printer Paper   or   Magazine Paper

Questions for Activity

- Why does the dart stop?
  It only has as much force as we give it.

- What force makes the dart stop?
  Gravity.

- Is gravity pulling it down or pushing it down?
  Gravity is a pulling force.

Once the rounds are complete, bring participants together and using an Excel spreadsheet and projector (a whiteboard could be used by hand) create a table of each participant's distances for the paper dart. Record distances in inches using the following format:

	Round 1	Round 2	Round 3
Participant 1	30	45	29
Participant 2	10	28	42

Excel: Highlight all of the data and select Insert→Scatter→Scatter with Only Markers. Your graph should look something like this:

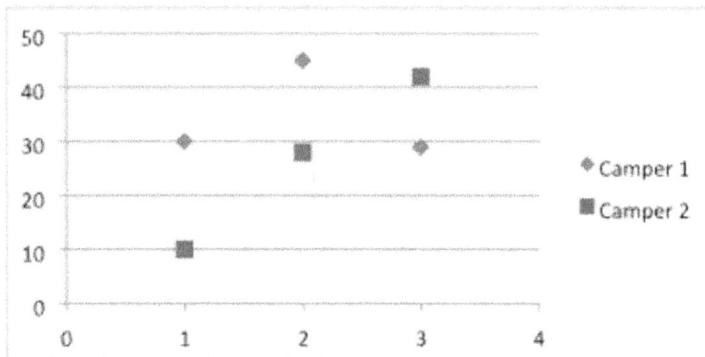

Ask participants what they think of this graph? What do they think it represents? What is the middle distance (This is called the median)? What is the longest distance? What is the shortest distance? Is there a distance that is repeated more than once? (This is called the mode) What round were these distances in?

Whiteboard: You can use the table written on the whiteboard, draw an axis and ask participants to come up to the board and plot their points (You may have to demonstrate how this is done). After the graph is drawn you can ask the same questions (above).

Note to Coach: Be sure to make the graphing activity an engaging activity with questions about the group's distances and how they relate to force and Newton's laws.

7.2: Preparing for the Future: AI Integration & Recap

Time Required	**20 min**
Group Sizes	**1 - 2**
Grade	**PreK - 5**

Learning Objectives
- Explore age-appropriate AI & machine learning to enhance understanding of motion & machines.

Here is a curated list of age-appropriate Artificial Intelligence (AI) / Machine Learning (ML) extensions that naturally build on Module 7 Mechanical Engineering lessons. These are designed to be optional enhancements, scalable from PreK through Grade 5, and aligned with your focus on motion, machines, data, and design thinking.

7.1 The Dart Challenge
- Motion Memory Chatbot (Grades PreK–5)
  - AI Skill: Recall & concept reinforcement
  - Before flying darts, students interact with a teacher-guided chatbot that asks:
    - "What makes something start moving?"
    - "What makes it stop?"
    - "What happens when you use more force?"
  - The chatbot reinforces Newton's Laws using simple language and examples from prior modules.

- Prediction Bot: How Far Will It Fly? (Grades PreK–5)
  - AI Skill: Prediction & hypothesis testing
  - Before each throw, students tell a chatbot or teacher-entered tool:
    - How hard they plan to throw
    - Whether they think it will go farther or shorter than last time
  - After the throw, students compare predictions to results and discuss why.

- Force Slider Simulation (Grades K–5)
  - AI Skill: Cause-and-effect modeling
  - Create a simple animation where a slider controls "force" and a dart travels different distances.
    - Recommended: Scratch
  - Discuss:
    - What changes when force increases?
    - How computers simulate motion using rules and variables

- Dart Data Collection + AI Charts (Grades 2–5)
  - AI Skill: Data analysis & visualization
  - Input dart distances and times into:
    - Bar graphs (distance per round)
    - Scatter plots (force vs distance)
  - Explain that AI looks at graphs like this to find patterns.

- Median / Mode Finder Tool (Grades 3–5)
  - AI Skill: Statistical pattern recognition
  - Use a spreadsheet or AI tool to automatically identify:
    - Median distance
    - Most common distance (mode)
    - Longest and shortest throws
  - Discuss why averages help computers make predictions.

- Paper vs Magazine Dart Comparison Model (Grades 3–5)
  - AI Skill: Feature comparison & classification
  - Students label throws by material type:
    - Printer paper
    - Magazine paper
  - Create a chart comparing distances.
  - Explain how ML compares features (material, weight, stiffness) to outcomes.

- Throw Consistency Analyzer (Grades 4–5)
  - AI Skill: Variability detection
  - Students examine:
    - How consistent their throws are
    - Which round had the biggest changes
  - Explain that AI notices inconsistency and uses repeated trials to improve accuracy.

- Motion Replay & Analysis (Teacher-Led, Grades 3–5)
  - AI Skill: Computer vision (conceptual)
  - Record a dart flight on a tablet or phone and replay in slow motion.
    - Recommended: https://teachablemachine.withgoogle.com/
  - Discuss how AI can:
    - Track movement frame by frame
    - Measure speed and direction over time

- Design Improvement Chatbot (Grades 4–5)
  - AI Skill: Iteration & optimization
  - After reviewing data, students ask:
    - "How could I improve my next throw?"
    - "What worked best before?"
  - Connect improvements to how AI learns from past attempts to perform better next time.

- Human vs AI Thinking Reflection (Grades 4–5)
  - AI Skill: Metacognition
  - Discuss:
    - How students decide how hard to throw
    - How a computer would decide using data
  - Highlight similarities between scientific thinking and machine learning.

Notes

www.ingramcontent.com/pod-product-compliance
Lightning Source LLC
Chambersburg PA
CBHW080427270326
41929CB00018B/3187